THE VOICE OF

MUSE _

UNARIUS _

ELYSIUM

Ernest L. Norman
Author, philosopher, poet, scientist, direc-
tor, moderator of Unarius Science of Life.

THE

VOICE OF MUSE

Clairvoyantly Received

By

Ernest L. Norman

***

The Fifth Volume of

THE PULSE OF CREATION

***

*

Published by
UNARIUS, SCIENCE OF LIFE
P.O. Box 1042
El Cajon, Calif. 92020

Notation

Footsteps of every Unariun student are well marked by the wonderful testimonials, miraculous happenings which graphically depict their ever changing metamorphosis in their ascension into a higher world. Yet of all these, no one is more miraculous than the life and death struggle of Helen Moore, following what would ordinarily have been, to other people, a fatal accident; yet Helen lived. She came back from that healing and convalescent period in a spiritual world to begin to complete the avowed and dedicated task of self development and service to humanity. How well she has accomplished this and how great her miracle is has been amply portrayed in her work in typing the sheets of these latest three books of the Pulse of Creation series; and this book therefore shall remain forever a testimonial of her miracle.

* * *

(The word 'trance' mentioned here is not meant in any sense, as the earth man's concept of some unconscious or hypnotic state, but rather is an inner attunement. E.L.N. is at all times fully aware and conscious. The word trance means transcended.)

PREFACE

In presenting to you these last three books of the Pulse of Creation series, we do so with our usual 'no reservation' policy, just as the other books have been so presented. However, in all fairness to we, the Unariun Brotherhood, and especially to you, dear student, we must therefore reinstate the entire policy and structure which applies to these seven Pulse of Creation books.

Like all others, these books were dictated (in trance) by means of tape recordings by the actual psychic personalities of those who have so identified themselves in the different chapters of these books. However, it must be explained to you that these are not the physical personalities as you may have had them depicted for you in history books, photos or pictures, etc., but rather, they are best described as stated, psychic personalities.

In order to best understand, let us go back for a moment to our lesson on the psychic anatomy, and especially to the development of the higher psychic embodiment known as the Superconscious Self. As stated, this Higher Self is constructed of the more positive inspirational and constructive manifestations or experiences in an individual's life. These are polarized with more positive facsimilies which reside in Infinite Consciousness sometimes called the fourth dimension, etc.

Now when this psychic embodiment or Higher Self develops to the point in its evolution of many thousands of years and through hundreds of earth lives, it can and does begin to become a separate personality, and further development in this direction will eventually lead to a more ultimate point wherein it is the complete and whole self, and no longer needs to live or remanifest through an earth life consciousness.

The seven great Centers described in these books are the somewhere in between worlds for these psychic

·personalities who have developed to the point where a more or less independent life has begun to be lived by them. They are quite capable of living this Higher World life providing two important juxtapositions are met. In other words, they must live this spiritual life in a somewhat similar and familiar way as it was lived and experienced in the earth world. The houses, streets, buildings, etc., even though they were constructed entirely of radiant energies, all of these adjutants so common to life were necessary as oscillating agents to make a conscious life possible for these psychic personalities; and yet in many instances, many of them maintained and manifested to some degree an earth life through a physical person, an example of one personality who was once known as Abraham Lincoln and who, at the time of this transmission into the book was reliving psychically his earth life through John Kennedy. So while Abraham Lincoln as a psychic personality was able to come through or project himself through the Moderator and his vocal cords in dictation, yet this psychic personality was not the physical personality as it was lived by Abe Lincoln one hundred years ago.*

Therefore, any such dictations either by him or by any other psychic personalities may not necessarily meet all of the supposedly classical requirements of the physical form. These personalities give their philosophies, their descriptions, etc., based on a memory consciousness of their earth life experiences in previous lifetimes and as they were so polarized in this Higher Consciousness. Sometimes these psychic personalities are able to project a strong phenomenon such as was the case with William James, the psychologist, who filled the room at the time of transmission with the pungent aroma of cigar smoke (very strongly choking the Moderator and Ruth also). This same cigar smoke has been projected to other students at the time or reading the transmission by James; in one case, several thousand miles away the student smelled it.

Now you begin to see and understand, dear student, why it is that through these Pulse of Creation books, you can walk through the corridors of time and you can see depicted in these great Centers all known civilizations, a factual cross section of life as it has been lived by man on this planet earth from the beginning, and you can see it all in the radiant irridescent colors of crystalline energy.

Through ancient Egypt and the dynasties of the Pharoahs, Amenhotep who in his time and in his language taught the interdimensional science of Unarius; or to ancient Greece and at the time of Anaxagoras who, through Pericles, designed and built the Acropolis and the Parthenon and the democratic civilization of that time. Yes, and he also presented the first atomic theory, the first comprehensive structure of mass.

Or you can stroll through other great Centers of culture and learning of arts and sciences. Yes, and some of them may be strange to you, for they are not part of the history of this earth, but come from other planets where mankind is also developing along these well described lines of evolution into a metamorphosis into a spiritual being.

So question not that these transmissions as they represent chapters in these books were delivered by those who so identified themselves, for indeed they were, even much more highly developed and intelligent than are their earth life counterparts who are depicted in history. And even as they spoke through the vocal chords of an earth man, this too, was not an easy matter for in the gutteral sounds of an animal world they tried to depict the beauty of their world, the great spiritual awareness of their existence, the completeness and the allness of this higher world; and if there are any apparent omissions in your mind, then try to place yourself in their position and to form that beautiful spiritual world into a few hundred words, or try to encompass your broadened understanding of Infinity with some earth-like comparisons.

Yes, indeed, as you can see they have all done well, and with their efforts they have also brought a great blessing — a full measure of transcendent power. And beyond these worlds are even greater Kingdoms wherein some long future time you too may live; Kingdoms which defy descriptions of any kind, for they contain none of the more familiar symbologies of the material world. There are none of the mountains, plains, skies or rivers; there are no churches or fake religious systems to point guilty fingers and reminders of evil. There are no governments to create wars or destroy civilizations; instead consciousness of each individual is attuned to the vast constructive Infinity. The mind beats with the pulse of creation. There are no degrading emotionalisms but a complete sense of living in a fullest and highest creative sense with none of the debased procreative sex drives.

So be it then, to your future, to your strength and to your will to survive the temptation which your own ignorance will flount before you for the tempter is always there. The devil incarnate who lives in the personality you have developed in the past and only the strongest faith can survive this seemingly everlasting tempter.

Like the hairs on your head the days of your earth life are numbered just as are all other lives so lived or to be lived for in the earth world the cycle of life is constantly divided by time; yet time in itself and in the completeness of all time do we find Infinity.

*A complete evaluation of comparisons between the lives of the two men, Abe Lincoln and J. F. Kennedy, has been prepared and will be sent (gratis) upon receipt of your request.

CHAPTER LXXXVIII

Dear ones. This is Athena. May we now resume our transmission. As you are now seemingly hovering above the great planet Muse, having left the Center of Parhelion, we are about to resume our exploration in this great City of Helianthus. While your eyes are becoming accustomed to the brilliance of the astral world about you, we will discuss somewhat the previous transmission which was given by the identity of Buddha.

The presentation of this individual as he came to you may, to certain individuals, produce a reaction of incredulity. It is to further enlarge these concepts or to clear up some elements of doubt which may arise in the minds of truth seekers that I shall try in the best way possible to reinstate certain concepts within the individual's mind. In the general presupposition of spiritual continuity, as it is expressed in the various evolutions of mankind and in the numerous histories, a great deal of the context of material relates either to spirit manifestation or to such apparitions which gave proper guidance, direction, or instructions to certain individuals who were thus so concerned.

The Holy Bible of your time makes numerous references to Celestial Beings appearing to various individuals who were transpiring their earth lives at that time. It is a much more natural and direct sequence and conclusion of spiritual truth or spiritual supplication to know that the higher Celestial or Causal Beings can more easily manifest themselves in the terrestrial dimensions in which concepts are related to your present knowledge of spiritualism than do the other types of spiritual communications. The average entity or discarnate being, as he is traveling in the world of maya or spirit in the subastral realms or dimensions is, in himself, quite unproductive and unrelative in his expression. It is quite difficult for him, even within the contact of the realm of frequency relationship, to reestablish a definite relationship with the earth, even though he may be very desirous of doing so. The elements which transpire here are, in a sense of the word, mediumistic and are not the proper elements of mental and spiritual relationship which must exist in the higher orders of spiritual transmission.

The whole idea or field of introspection which relates man to the conscious continuity with his Higher Self is one which involves a great deal of study. We might point out that numerous individuals have, as they believe at different times in psychic transitions in their lives, so seen manifestations of Christ; and it was previously pointed out that usually such appearances of psychic phenomena merely related to the actual seeing of the personal embodiments of the Higher Self, which developed into the personal idea of the Christ within the individual. However, it is quite apparent too that this Christ idea is merely the relationship of the Higher Self to the Infinite Mind of God, just as it was with the Avatar Jesus. He constituted the personal relationship of the Higher Self with the Infinite Nature to such a degree that He was able to constitute His miraculous expression of spiritual transition in every dimension. It is within this mistaken concept, or I shall say that people so confounded the relationship of the Christ Self that they believe Jesus and Christ to be God; and while this is true, in a sense of the word, yet it must be properly separated or segregated into the personal relationship basis, otherwise we would be wandering in a maze of intricate relationships or beliefs which would have no fundamental concept.

As it was pointed out by Gautama, his own interpretation of spiritual law, order, and integration was one which was very simple and monotheistic in nature. He taught the simple absolvence of the physical dimension around you, that it should be placed in its subservient relationship to the Higher Self, and in this self-realization of the Higher Self, one obtained Nirvana or the

950

relaxation from the nervous and physical tensions of the terrestrial world. Within the complete contemplation and assuredness of the affinity with God's Infinite Nature, man could progress into such other concepts as were more relative to the Universal Consciousness of the Brotherhood of man. The simplicity of Buddhism itself was a fertile field wherein were planted numerous seeds of pantheism which, as it later developed, so sprouted and grew and were nurtured by the different elemental interjections of spiritual interpretations into these Buddhistic concepts; so that, as it exists today, Buddhism is a far more vastly intricate and interwoven pantheism than it was as it existed at the time of Buddha.

The presentation of this vast complexity of ideology and spiritual form to the Western mind has created somewhat of a problem to the individual who is seeking to unravel or untangle the pure concepts of Truth as they are so contained. It is quite apparent that the Western mind believes that India is a country wherein thousands of people run around with their heads shaved and have various kinds of pins or hooks or other torturous devices impounded into their flesh, or that a great part of the population spend their sleeping or waking hours lying on beds of nails or being buried in the ground or such other numerous fallacious interpretations. Buddha, himself — in his mission during his life on earth — was somewhat shocked by these apparitions and derelictions of spiritual truths.

It can also be pointed out that the missions of the seven different Avatars, as they have appeared or reappeared at different times in the dimensions of the terrestrial earth, and the philosophies they taught have been quite similar in their general delivery and context. Just as it was in Buddhism, so it was with Jesus; His pure monotheistic doctrine of simplicity

951

was so warped, maligned, and distorted into the various thousands of numerous interpretations of what is called Christianity in your world today. The Ten Commandments of Buddha today are somewhat similar to the Ten Commandments of Moses; and they, in turn, if one seeks to analyze thoroughly the spiritual elements in any of these so-called laws, present certain spiritual presentations quite similar to the Beatitudes which were given by Jesus. All of the elements of Truth were so contained therein, in somewhat of the lines of demarcation which is the proper interpretation of any law.

God Himself has no laws, as He is what might be called 'Law'. The word law, itself, is rather confusing in its nature as it divides a certain circumscribed dimension of relationship or concept, or that such concept can extend in the definite confines of a certain circumscribed dimension. As God is Infinite in nature, it is not logical to try to confine God in any finite dimension or what is called the circumscribed order of law as is expressed from a material dimension. The fact of the matter is that an individual can only perceive law, order, and harmony as he progresses into the spiritual dimensions. Such orders of law as they are expressed in a terrestrial dimension are, by necessity, extremely conflicting and are, in themselves, multiple in nature; the observance of these laws will tend to lead the individual far astray from his path of true progression.

The true simple monotheistic doctrine of Jesus — as you will see in the course of study of history in its development from the time of Paul — has developed into the Holy Roman Empire a pantheism which was, in some respects, quite similar to the so-called Buddhistic concepts as they have existed in India for countless thousands of years; and they have also existed in China and Japan. The ritualism which is involved in such concepts is quite similar to that which has existed in the Roman Catholic version of Christianity since its inception at the time of Paul. This was so because the elements of such ritualism were expressed not only through the Mythraic concepts as they were interwoven into Christianity, but minds of men became fouled with the interpretation of the presence of the physical flesh so that these principles were not properly translated.

We could further enlarge this concept as it was the same principle of strangulation which entered into the interpretation of the Parable of the Garden of Eden; and here again, man's mind became fouled with that same projection of physical consciousness. As it was previously explained, man was portrayed entering into the terrestrial dimensions as the opposite or divided polarities of himself, and that he would merely view the creation and the evolution of himself into the higher dimensions from two exact opposite polarities. It did not mean that man, in his opposite polarities, was either good or evil, but that he was merely viewing all things and creating experience within himself and absorbing the nature or the value of such experience introspectively in regard to the different dimensions of his polarity; and in unification of this polarity into the Celestial Dimensions or the Causal World, he again becomes an activated or a participating principle of God's Infinite nature.

Now, you have become somewhat accustomed to looking down upon the great City of Helianthus as it was so previously described as a huge Central Temple which could house many millions of people, and stemming from this huge Central Temple were the thirty-three great radial sections of the city which were somewhat like the petals of the sunflower. The concept of astrophysics here, as it is so contained within the structure of the city, must be somewhat entered into before you can properly evaluate the entire correct law of order and harmony in the expression of the terrestrial dimension which you call your earth, as it so exists in other planetary systems.

As Buddha said, there are the thirty-three Logi or spiritual dimensions of the Causal world which are reflecting down, or we shall say, they are in conjunction with the Infinite Mind of God in radiating a benign order of Light or frequency of energy into the lower dimensions, so that you shall see in your explorations of these different dimensions, thirty-three sections; they in themselves, relate to thirty-three different basic interpretations of cyclic order as it exists in the histories of your terrestrial dimensions, and as such, they exist there for countless other planets in different other terrestrial dimensions which are around in this part of the galaxy of the universe. These thirty-three benign rays or paths of Light, as they are so related into the regular order of procession or cycles, are in uniform order and conjunction with the Infinite cyclic order from the Mind of God. They so unify the personal relationship of man with his higher order of evolution. In turn, these orders of frequency relationship are so divided and subdivided into different orders of frequency relationship. The second order which we will consider is of the number twelve as you have thus twelve months in your year, so that this great cycle of thirty-three thousand years is properly divided by the multiple of the denominator of two and one-half times, which is the frequency relationship in the third dimension. Then the thirty-three thousand years are roughly divided into twelve segments of a little over two thousand years duration. The exact number of years is, in itself, not too important, as there are several derivations of the quotient of time as it is so contained in the Celestial dimensions.

Coming down through the evolutions through the hundreds of thousands of years since the time of Shamballa in India, the translations of the Vedas contained a great cycle of twenty-four thousand years which was in itself, as they believed, the transition of man from the lowest to the highest, and from the highest to the lowest states of consciousness. This did not, if you will think for a moment, relate any individual to this twenty-four thousand year cycle. It merely meant that the stream of mankind would pass through such a cycle. This seems to be somewhat of an apparent contradiction to the thirty-three thousand year cycle; but they are actually one and the same, and the element of twenty-four thousand years is merely the resolution which was developed from the quotients of time or their interpretations into such calendric systems of the interpretation of time and in their derivatives through the countless evolutions from the time of Shamballa into the Vedic translations. The same principle is interjected into your Gregorian calendar.

Your modern physicist relates this same great cycle of thirty-three thousand years into what he calls the cycle of the recessional, which, to him, according to his Gregorian calendar, is 25,862 years. From the dimension in which we live, it appears in relationship to your earth time, and as it developed into the Essenic Orders of Brotherhood and the Gnostics, or to the builders of the pyramids in Egypt that the correct number of years is about thirty-three thousand (33,000).

This order, too, is manifest in the Masonic relationships which are derivatives from the old Essenic or Gnostic cults as they existed on the earth at one time. Do not be confused by the element of time or to the interjection of years according to your Gregorian calendar, nor to such other suppositions of calendric systems as they have existed on the earth at different times. The element of time, in itself, is merely cyclic in fashion and it truly developed into its higher dimension from where your concept of time does not really exist.

It is in that cyclic form and in manifesting a cyclic

pattern, it thus manifests a continual procession of infinities, which is the compound essence of time in God's own Infinite Nature. Just as this Infinite Mind so impounded within your own original superconsciousness of your life cycle the infinite aspects of Its nature, so thus in direct proportion you will, in traveling about this cycle, never come to the end of the time or place where there are not new manifestations or revelations; or where there are not new concepts which continually resolve into your dimension of relationship with the Infinite Mind.

This, in itself, will be a constant procession or a parade whereby you will thus, as we have told you, link and relink yourself with the countless millions of Infinite harmonic structures which exist throughout God's intelligent universe, whether it be Celestial, Cosmic, or terrestrial. The actual exploration of these thirty-three different sections will, in themselves, entail a good deal of what might be called repetitious reproductions of different aspects of life as they have been so contained in the history books or in the elements of the passing of the different epochs in the evolution of man on the earth.

There are likewise contained therein numerous reproductions of epochs of time which relate to other earths and to other terrestrial systems. We shall find, if it is not too confusing, that they may also contain certain elements in the transition of evolution into some of the other orders of astral worlds which are, shall I say, somewhat in a lower vibrating order than that in which we exist here in Helianthus. So, all in all, I could say that the mere exploration of the city will be one which could, in a future day of your evolution, involve something like several thousand years of earth time. It is quite obvious that to implant even a small fraction of what is contained in this vast city into the lines and pages of your book would be physically impossible nor shall we attempt to do so. We are more concerned that you become more acquainted with the working principles which are contained in the expression of this vast city and into the natural sequence of order and relationship in the various comings and goings of the different individuals who are so concerned and related into their own dimension of frequency interpretation.

I see that I have been progressing somewhat too rapidly for a proper interpretation from the mental to the physical form of speech. I shall, therefore, halt my rapid progress of words to something which will be more easily deciphered. As we have been talking, we have somewhat descended into a closer proximity of this great Central Temple which you see directly beneath you. Here again are the striking appearances of these Radiant Celestial Energies as they have been described on their different multiplicities of dimensional forms in your previous explorations.

The Temple here is, just as others, unique in its own design and construction. It was so conceived, not only from the viewpoint of beauty, but it was also conceived into a more utilitarian pattern. The basic part of this temple is a huge circular dome-shaped structure, and there are thirty-three regularly interspersed doorways or huge arched openings which are somewhat Gothic in appearance, which exactly intersect the different radial buildings and seem to stem out in the heliocentric fashion from this temple. Between these buildings, however, is a vast courtyard which is landscaped and contains numerous pools and plantings of the different shrubbery, flowers, and trees which, as in the other worlds, are so abundant and reproduced in a more spiritual form of beauty and outward countenance. They sparkle and are colored with the iridescent beauty of the rainbow; and while a plant may be said to be green, yet it cannot be said that it is not also one of many other hues. It seems, in a sense, to be very intelligent toward you, and you can actually hear it, in a somewhat vague way, communicate to you something of the beauty of the energies with which it is so constructed.

These things are, in themselves, sort of a telepathic communion or a realization within the inner confines of your own mind, and you are so completely absorbed and saturated with the beauty which is all about you that you become infused with the aesthetic nature of God's inner Self. You are buoyant and jubilant, and you feel revitalized; you feel completely compensated in all directions of thought, and there is a vast unity or a progression of law, order and harmony within you. The different vicissitudes of the earthly life have vanished and the world of maya is no longer about you. You see in the radiant pulsating energies and these beautiful structures which are about you a more factual demonstration of the higher principles which are contained within the mind of the Infinite Nature of man himself in his relationship to the Infinite God. However, I see that your vocal cords are becoming tired and enmeshed somewhat; so for the present moment we shall rest until a further continuance. In God's Love.
— Athena.

CHAPTER LXXXIX

Greetings to my dear earth brothers and sisters; may I first say that I am so happy to come to you and to be of some service to you. I can be known in the future as the personal identity of a small Chinaman who lived about a hundred years after Kung Fu, and was known as Mencius or Meng Tse. I have been given the privilege of conducting you through this great city of Helianthus; and we are about ready to somewhat explore the sections which are more immediately concerned with your earth history. However, before we go into this section, we shall pause in this beautiful parkway and discuss something more of the philosophies of Hinduism while your eyes are becoming accustomed to what you see about you.

The text of Buddha, in itself, was simply one which he largely devoted to the explanation of the origin of the different phases of Hinduism as they exist much as they do in India today. He was, during his earth life, very greatly shocked at seeing the suffering of the peoples who believed they were practicing the true monistic God Principles by this perversion and abuse of their bodies. The version of the Brahmanistic concepts or the Vedic translations as they have been so warped and distorted were completely vilified in many ways by the individual known as Brahavara, the person who became known as the god Janus. Buddha pointed this out specifically, knowing that no harm would come from this direct finger pointing at this individual, because he knows that this person has, since that time, come into a place of spiritual understanding; and although he did set aside the divine conception of Brahma — the triad of Brahma, Vishnu and Shiva — yet, since that day, he has worked out and expiated his crime, and was enabled to reincarnate into your world and was known as the Mahatma Gandhi.

So now you see that while we may have been ostracized very definitely for criticizing an individual, yet

959

it was not the individual we criticized, but rather the work that person did while he was on the earth. The whole superconsciousness of the individual, as you see, went through a great metamorphosis in a spiritual dimension, and so he completely worked out his karma by serving mankind in a very large and in a very humble capacity. Buddha, himself, is a very humble person; he did not very fully enlarge upon the simplicity of the spiritual concepts as he so tried to teach them on the earth at that time. Buddhism, as it existed some time after his death and as it still exists today, was not strictly the philosophy which he taught, but just as in the case of Christianity, the various concepts suffered a great deal of distortion in recurring as a definite philosophy in the future years of evolution. Buddha did little or no writing, himself, but was followed about by a number of disciples or apostles just as was Jesus.

One of these persons was a very avid disciple by the name of Upolia. It was Upolia who became known as the St. Paul of Buddha and it was he who wrote the numerous transcripts known as the 'Tripitaka', or the 'Three Baskets of Bread', wherein were contained the Ten Commandments of Buddha. If you will note the first one which says, "Thou shalt not kill any living thing"; this was an old Brahmanical concept which had been handed down through the Vedic laws. Buddha was very temperate in all his philosophies. He said, "Thou shalt not kill", but he meant, "Thou shalt not kill thy brother or sister"; and there were other distortions, or shall I say different interminglings of various kinds of personal ideas into the original Buddhistic concept. If you will read your history books, you will see that Jesus, like Buddha, did not come into his expression of Christianity until the time of Constantine, who, at that time, established what was to become the Roman Catholic Church, and contributed to the reestablishing of the Byzantine Empire, or to filling the original concept as it was so begun in Greece.

The parallel here with Buddhism is very marked; the concept of Buddha was known only locally in his own province, and it did not come into its own until about three hundred years later under the reign of King Asoka, who became a very devout follower of Buddha and succeeded in propagating this concept into the far reaches of India. Hinduism or Buddhism, as it exists in India today, is a very strong intermingling of all the old concepts of Brahminisms and the Triad of Brahma as it existed, including the various types of pantheism which are known as Jainism, and the different interpretations of Buddha. You might say that India is universally under one flag or banner; they all have somewhat the same intermingling of concept, and during these many thousands of years since, have become thoroughly intermingled. You will notice also that many of the early travelers in India were quite surprised to see the Christian cross and other symbols which were used in Buddhism or in the concepts of Hinduism. This was simply because that intercourse or traveling was carried on throughout the many thousands of years; and India was not, as was commonly supposed, completely isolated from the Western world.

The Greeks, the Jews, and the Egyptians very often came into India in the various caravans or perhaps they came individually and so carried with them, not only some of the ritualism and beliefs of their own native country, but also carried back to these same countries some of the beliefs of the Hinduism or Buddhism as they had so seen and witnessed in the various ceremonies.

Now, just a word more about the concept of, shall I say, astrophysics, as it was somewhat explained to you in a previous transmission of the thirty-three radial dimensions as they are expressed from the Great Central Temple here. You will see certain insignia above the great entrance ways into these different thirty-three sections. The sections themselves relate to the periods or cycles of one thousand years as they are portrayed in magnetic line structures of the solar system in which you are now residing. The solar system is so linked and counterlinked with the Central Vortex of the great universe. The one-thousand year cycles are conjunctions of spiritual force of these thirty-three centers wherein renewed impingements or modulations of spiritual nature are intermingled with these magnetic lines of structures. The task of further propagating or stimulating spiritual guidance and growth of mankind upon the earth and into other places of the galaxy, known as the universe, is carried on in the twelve subdivisions or sections which we manifest here from this Shamballa. They, in turn, take up this work in these twelve divisions which are actually about two-thousand seven-hundred and fifty years. These sections, in themselves, are somewhat of the astrological nature or interpretation as they have been so devised upon the earth plane. They will start from Pisces and continue on around through Aquarius. All in all, it can be said to be a very cleverly devised way in which these great minds have so conceived to interject the various spiritual knowledge and wisdom and to further enhance the value of man's progression in the lower dimensions.

This is somewhat in the form of personal intercession, as it might be said, in that these very strong spiritual rays are constantly within the superconsciousness of the individuals as they reside in these lower dimensions. However, I do believe that in the future you will evaluate these concepts in your own way and in your own mind.

Now let us go directly into this first great section, which you see has over the doorway, as part of the insignia, two very strange-looking forms of fishes which have their tails entwined about each other; they seem to be standing on their tails with their mouths open wide, and they have huge staring eyes. This, the sign of Pisces, denotes the two states of consciousness within the concept of man, his karmic or material state of consciousness and his spiritual state of consciousness. We can be assured that which we find within this temple will be, at least, mostly associated with the earth and its evolution within the last two thousand years. However, for purposes of further including or intermingling these different concepts, much within each of these temples is sometimes duplicated within one or another of the other sections. This is for the purpose, as you will see, of acquainting the many large groups of the many thousands of students who remain within these great sections for many hundreds of years or until they have assimilated the knowledge which is necessary for them to progress further.

Now that we are directly inside, the first sight which greets your eye is a huge Hindu temple. You, dear sister and brother, saw such a picturization on your TV screen quite recently, and we can enlarge this concept; as you can see, it does bear somewhat the same resemblance of the numerous and intricate maze of spires and various other types of very finely devised symbols which are on the outside of this great edifice. This temple is called the Temple of Manu, or the law maker. It was Manu who so brought, conceived, and interwove into the original Vedic transcripts the concept of Brahma, Vishnu, and Shiva. Brahma, as you know, is the Infinite Conception; he is supposed to be the great Celestial or Causal world of spiritual interpretation. Vishnu is the more immediate or pranic world which was symbolized as a great god who lived from the sun. It was Shiva who became the giver of life, or that from Shiva was expressed the numerous karmic laws of reincarnation. The spiritual as well as the physical nature of man was contained within these concepts of reincarnation. Coming down through the many hundreds of years, or even thousands of years since the time of Manu, these concepts were so warped and distorted within man's consciousness that much of their purity and spiritual virtue was lost.

Man contrives into himself, through the numerous complexes of guilt which were incurred in his nature, to change these concepts to suit his own taste or purpose. This is a universal custom and is not completely confined to the concepts of Hinduism. The same practice goes on in all churches and in all synagogues on the earth today. Man is continually changing the innermost divine concepts to something which he can orient within his own way of life or thinking, or that he can so expiate some sense of guilt within himself by saying that God has punished him, or that he might say, "Ho, I need not worry. Jesus will save me, etc."

This great temple, as you see, seems to be glittering with gold; it is indeed some such material in its very highly developed spiritual form. The various intricate sculpturings and carvings which cover the outside surface of this great temple, the small figures and gargoyles, the fishes; these, and the infinite number of types of symbols as they are so fabricated are, in themselves, pageantry of history; and they are also devised in many of the temples of India today. The meanings of these symbols and the portent which is contained therein have been lost in antiquity. The Hindu of today does not know how to interpret the spiritual meanings of the numerous figures which he handed down from generation to generation. He has no knowledge of carving or so contriving these figures in the walls of his temples; he does not know how to correctly translate them. Within this temple you will find the numerous translations of the original Vedic texts as

964

they were so contained at the time of migration from the plane of Mongolia. These texts were extracts or derivations of the spiritual truths which were handed down to man from the old original Shamballa which existed on the great crystal plateau in Central Mongolia.

So, all in all, you can see that the modern concepts of Hinduism bear only a small resemblance to the original spiritual philosophy which was so handed down to man from this great Shamballa. Such context of material is necessarily confined in its expression and in its nature into something which man has conceived to be purposes of self-punishment or infliction, or that he must adopt and stand for many hours in different postures, or lay in cramped positions, or to such supposedly inducive meditative processes whereby he can communicate with his inner nature. We would like to point out that these concepts, as they are so contained in the expression of Hinduism in your time, are not, in the general sense of the word, entirely practical to the working out in your world or sphere of reincarnation. Nor, could you so properly work out any karmic influence which is contained in your past histories by so sitting for many hours in constant meditation upon the inner nature.

While we say that a great degree of consciousness within this inner nature, or inner self is of the utmost importance; yet this should not be set aside, nor should the individual delete the purposes of his incarnation into the earth. It must be remembered that according to the laws of frequency relationship in the various cycles in which the karma was incurred, that the individual subconsciously comes into the time and place when these karmic conditions will be remanifested into his life in such a way that he will be able to largely rectify them by suffering some sort of a small psychic shock wherein the elements of different time consonants are of such nature that it also aids in rectifying these conditions of impingements or wave forms in his psychic body. You can reasonably see that any one who would sit upon the temple steps for weeks and years in a meditative position would not be in such a conducive phase of his life whereby he could work out these different karmic structures in his psychic anatomy.

The world of maya, or the material world about you, is one which was largely conceived, and of which you largely conceived yourself to be a part; and so in working through these different dimensions of maya or illusions, you incurred these karmic conditions. It is your purpose to come back into these different worlds until you have progressed to such a point where you can become more dominant with these conditions, and that you can more thoroughly regulate the progression of cycles in your own earth life. This begins your evolution into the higher dimensions.

The posture of meditation and inward consciousness were meant primarily, or they should be exercised only by individuals who were called Yogis. These individuals had, in themselves, a complete state of dominion of consciousness, so that they could — through these meditative processes — completely separate themselves from their physical bodies at any time which they so chose. I might point out that these practices are very dangerous for the initiate or to the person who is not thoroughly familiar with the ways and the knowledge of spiritual transformation, for he could incur a great deal of trouble and run afoul of some very definite spiritual obsessions if he so entered into such practices without being thoroughly schooled in such practices before he indulged in them.

If you were to go to India today, you would see many people who go about with hooks and skewers in their bodies, and as they thought, were punishing themselves for some small infraction of the law or that they might be adopting the numerous torturous postures and remain seemingly suspended in a catalytic state for hours or days and even years at a time. Such an individual is, in himself, and to a large degree, simply stopping his spiritual evolution. He has come to the point where the various guilt complexes in his nature were so strong that he must retreat into some sort of psychic trance, wherein he believes that he is working out his salvation. This is contrary to the law of frequency relationship, in working out these karmic conditions which incurred the guilt complexes.

It was Buddha who tried to teach that such practices were contrary to the general law, and, in so teaching, he aroused a great deal of resentment; he had to so modify his teachings which would somewhat conform with the general ideas and practices as they existed in his time. The mere idea of teaching people to discard caste systems, as they had been in their social structures for thousands of years, was, in itself, something which aroused a great deal of antagonism. Therefore, Buddha had to more or less float with the stream in order to sow the seed which he hoped would develop into a more factual philosophy. So you see, dear ones, that in India, even though it is a land of strange mystery and strange cults and practices, these practices of cultisms, of Brahma, and Hinduism, as they are expressed as religions, are not entirely practical nor are they entirely without the element of error.

These elements of error are so contained in all of the religions of the world; they are contained in Christianity, in Judaism and in many other interpretations of life. There is, at present, a third dimension of expression which is trying to sweep through the world and overpower all such spiritual concepts; and while these spiritual concepts, as they exist today in your world, are with some fault, yet they are, in themselves, very necessarily contributing factors in elements of spiritual progression to the individual. He may incur some karma or he may, as we say, learn to devote himself into such forms of altar worship which he may have to unlearn in some future time and age. But purely, in a sense of the word, he is gradually working toward that time of his evolution when he becomes a dominant spiritual personality in harmony with the Infinite Consciousness into some of the higher astral worlds.

There are — while you are watching and looking about at this great temple of Manu and noticing the beautiful mosaic tiled floors — the great statues of the different gods as they are so manifest in India today, and you can further describe these scenes to your fellow earth man. We will progress somewhat along the lines of modern psychiatry as they are expounded in the medical translations of inductive therapies in the fields of psychology and psychiatry of your day. Anyone who is studying such philosophies or interpretation is, as a consequence, subject to a vast amount of different interpretations of what is called psychological or psychiatric material. The elements entering into such philosophies, as they are so numerous, must be, in direct contrast, quite confusing — and indeed they are.

The tides of expression as they have arisen from the middle ages, from the days in which people were burned at the stake for witchcraft — for merely conceiving some of the more mental and spiritual natures of man — are now being expressed into your present day, as some of these exponents have become known as psychiatrists or doctors or psychologists. For the purposes of analytical evaluation we shall classify psychology into two divisions; the reactionary group which is by far the largest group, and the liberal expression or the progressive group. In the reactionary group will be found the very numerous doctors or practitioners as they exist in different hospitals, clinics, or private practice in the various cities about your world today. It is this reactionary group which is largely practicing such concepts of psychology or psychiatry which have more or less been practiced by such exponents as Freud, Watson, James, and others whose names are too numerous to mention. The Freudian concept, in itself, seems to be one which is in more popular usage. It is based primarily, as it was in Freud's time, upon two basic instincts, as he called them, the sexual nature and the will to survive. The modern psychologist has, however, modified these concepts to some extent. He immediately throws up his hands in horror at the mere mention of instinct. However, we might remind you that such facets that enter into the interpretation of psychology or psychiatry are not explained to any great extent in any concept of psychology or psychiatry as they exist today. The psychologist cannot tell you why it is that a child, almost from the time he starts to crawl, becomes somewhat destructive in his nature, and that he is continually trying to break up things about which he knows nothing. The psychologist may mutter something about a reflex or impounded reactions into the consciousness of the child, but these are not so easily brushed aside. The fact remains that most children, if they become destructive in their childhood, are m e r e l y reflecting from their psychic consciousness the little wave forms and vortexes which are impounded in the psychic body; the numerous manifestations of destructiveness, which they have, at some time in their evolution manifested in a reactionary way from some previous earth lives.

These destructive potentialities of the child's nature were not incurred either in one lifetime or in several lifetimes, but they are a conglomerate result of many reincarnations in a material domain which is largely reactionary in nature. So it can be said as

Freud said — a child as an individual reacts in a destructive manner toward anything which he does not understand, and that he tries to destroy such an appearance of some such object of truth or idea which he may encounter which is foreign to his understanding. Freud himself was, almost to the time of his passing, shaking his head and muttering that all mankind was too thoroughly steeped in the tradition of sex, and that his basic and motivating instincts were based upon the concepts of sex. Here again, just as Freud would tell you if he could be here talking with you, these concepts of sex — while they were basic and relative in certain dimensions of expression among individuals who had not yet worked out certain karmic obstructions in their natures — were a great and dominant factor in controlling the appearances of everyday life; but it was not by such necessity the extreme and controlling factor of evolution as it would so affect the individual in his future progression.

The liberal or progressive camp of psychiatry or psychology, too, does not embody too much of a general philosophy which can be considered to be, actually, of such nature which will further the progress of man in his present dimension. This camp of interpretation contains such elements of parapsychology as are expressed in the numerous psychical research bodies throughout America and throughout the various other countries of the world. Here again, while these elements are progressive in nature and the constituents contained therein are much of the spiritual nature of man, yet they too lack a certain fundamental element which is very necessary and vital to understand the more spiritual nature of man himself. If we pin a psychologist or a psychic researcher down to the point where he must actually explain — what is a reflex — what is an idea — what is an instinct — or what is an emotional experience — he cannot define just exactly what these things are. If we ask him where they are, he will point to the brain and say they are in the brain. He will point out that they have an instrument or mechanical robot which is called the encephalograph which is supposed to denote certain wave forms or electronic impulses which are supposed to stem from the brain. While this is so, yet he cannot — if you bring him directly to the point — actually define from whence this life force comes.

The physicist, the scientist, as well as the psychologist is today attempting, not only to put the contents of life in a test tube, but he can magnify it on the oscilloscope or make other interpretations. He can put life under a microscope and see it; he will not, nor can he ever build it and fabricate it according to his own will of consciousness. This is, in itself, a pure dominion of God's own spiritual consciousness, and the creative processes of creating man's spiritual nature are entirely within the concept of God Himself.

The net product of analyses which the psychologist or the scientist, or the psychiatrist is trying to define as life is, as we have so numerously interpreted and interjected in our transmissions, the fabrication of spiritual structure which is known as the psychic body and that it resides and lives in a dimension which is not physical in nature nor can it ever be determined in the pure quotient of the reactionary nomenclature or to such procedures of analytical psychology as are expressed in your world today. They must, as we have said, be interjected and fully explained in the field which is more closely related to parapsychology or that an entirely new science and interpretation must come into being which embodies the element of clairvoyance, or such psychic knowledge which will enable the practitioner to see, to sense, and to visualize and interpret in some way, into his analogies, such conditions, or of what the spiritual structures of man really consist.

The present day psychologist or the analyst, as he is practicing in the numerous clinics and hospitals and in the various private practices of the earth today, takes a great deal of pride in the fact that he can spew forth from his mouth a great deal of nomenclature which he denotes as the various types of mental aberrations and he has called them by such names as reflexes or factions of an inhibitive nature, or that they are neurotic or a paranoid or schizoid; or they may be other forms of mentally distorted or aberrated people to such an extent that they have lost a normal functional relationship with the world about them. Such terms and such nomenclature, in themselves, mean little or nothing, as any psychologist knows that no two patients ever exhibit exactly the same tendencies and relationships of these abnormal expressions in themselves. Each patient expresses a certain challenge wherein are contained certain elements of personal evaluation which are different from another; classifications of mental aberrations are just rather broadly defined conditions wherein a person may be generally classified.

In viewing psychology as it exists today upon the earth, you would see the numerous and entirely opposite translations of life in the various nations and communities of the world, and that the exact and extreme opposites of the interpretations of life are often very predominantly displayed so as a direct consequence, psychology must be extremely flexible in nature, and such extreme flexibility can only be equated into the dimensions of pure science, because pure science is absolute and inflexible. There are no elements in your physical or material science which cannot or could not be clearly defined in a mathematical formula, or to such equations as could be expressed in some of the electronic robots of your time.

The extreme nature of man as he is expressing in your world today, and as he does in other worlds — indicates, to a large degree, the infinite nature of man himself, and into such infinite concepts the psychologist or psychiatrist must, by direct consequence, relate man into higher dimensions of life or to his relative sequence of such evolution. You might think that such psychology would, in direct proportion, be of an extremely complex nature, but such is not so. If we remember the basic elements of psychic structures, and that in the expression of some clairvoyant diagnosis the individual can very thoroughly be diagnosed for such psychic impacts as have caused his mental aberration and his own states of evolution. Statistics will indicate, as they exist in the cities of the world today and especially in America, that the elements of the numerous types of physical diseases or mental conditions indicate that the number one problem of mankind is mental health. The problem of mental health, in itself, as it can be very clearly seen by such statistics and a further perusal of how this mental condition arrived at its staggering proportion will indicate that it is purely a product of the civilization in which you live.

There are numerous races and tribes of people living on the earth today who can be called savage or somewhat primitive in their expressions but you will notice that the rate of mental aberrations or that their rate of mental health is a comparatively very small fraction in direct comparison to that which is incurred by the average individual in the larger civilized cities of the world.

As any psychologist can tell you in your present day and age, even the little doggies in the household are very often quite neurotic, and children suffer from stomach ulcers which are often, in themselves, a symptom of a neurosis. Statistics indicate that in your America one person in ten is badly in need of corrective therapy, or that ten million are in such a condition of mental health that they are no longer useful in the communities where they live; and they have become by di-

rect consequence, to a large degree, somewhat dangerous. By such statistics we can also positively evaluate the present psychiatry or psychology as being of
little, if any, use in stemming the tide of negativity
which is warping and distorting the minds of the American people. In direct consequence, it must be
thoroughly understood that a new and entirely different
type of corrective therapy is in extreme and urgent
need at the present time.

Nor is the present psychology so related to another
aspect of the American way of life, and this psychiatry
should include this expression which is called the
criminal. The criminal is just as neurotic and just as
insane as any person who is confined in a mental institution. Your records will reveal that such criminals as
have been incarcerated and have been either pardoned
or placed back into society on parole have returned and
returned to the penal institutions; and as any psychologist can tell you, as they are characteristically and
predominantly criminal, they cannot, in any sense of
the word, be cured. I am referring to the large majority
of criminals who are impounded into such institutions.
There are, of course, some innocent victims and others
too, who will, in a future day, be able to regulate their
lives into a more useful sequence.

But, as a whole, the product of civilization which
is contained in the large cities is highly conducive to
the criminal elements which will badly warp and distort
the minds of the youngsters as they grow up so that
they become hardened reprobates and cannot, at the
time of their earth lives, ever become suitably or cor-
rectively instituted to some social structure. These
criminally aberrated conditions in these mentalities are
further complicated by the great seas of astral forces
which — as we have described them as individual enti-

ties — are swirling about in the aura of the earth. As a youngster is warped or distorted into some criminal propensity, so he always does, as a direct consequence, impound within his psychic nature the obsessive influences of the numerous astral entities who have, at some time in their earth lives, been criminals or mentally perverted in some way.

And here again you see the fallacious interpretation of corrective therapy by constructing the penal institutions or corrective reform schools and incarcerating these criminals together under a common roof. As they are so confined, others are attempting to impress them with the idea that they are wrong-doers. This is a very silly thing to do as the criminal himself is in no position to properly evaluate a constructive philosophy of life. Here again it must be borne in mind that corrective therapy, as far as the criminal would be concerned, should be one in which we would first remove from the cities of your civilization the elements which first warped or distorted or brought into the consciousness of the individual these criminal propensities.

The reactionary way of life in the environment of the slum elements and in the hurry and scurry, as has been called the 'rat race' of life on the planet earth in these large cities, is very highly productive of warping and distorting a child's mind. The father and mother themselves are often individuals who have been living on the fringeline of criminal propensities; and they may have, actually, from time to time, been guilty of misinterpretation of flagrantly violating the law of social structure, so that the child, as a consequence, has nothing in his environmental factors which is conducive to a more integrated and constructive spiritual or social way of life. It is one thing to live under a wonderful and beautiful idealistic concept, as was contained in the constitution, a free way of life to the average individual who so arrives in a great civiliza-

975

tion, such as America, but it is quite another thing to properly relate such individuals with spiritual concepts in the environmental factors of their daily lives that will enhance and propagate the necessary virtues of their natures so that they may become useful citizens.

This, in various ways, has been attempted by the inclusion of numerous churches, or the child will be sent to Sunday School, or to such other places where he can learn something of the spiritual and historical background of mankind. Or, he may be sent to some public school and taught the rudimentary factions as they are contained in the educational systems of your time. But these things, in themselves, while they are much better than having nothing at all, have not yet arrived at such a point where they can completely integrate a child into what could be a much more useful and highly developed way of his life.

The people on other planets have arrived at the conclusions of child psychology where they can properly evaluate the child's potentials in such a manner where he would further develop along the line for which he is most suited and adapted. Such other conditions, as are contained in his psychic body, must also be removed so that he does not continually suffer from the handicap of the psychic blocks which may exist in this psychic structure from other lifetimes.

However, these things are much in advance of your present day knowledge of psychology and psychiatry. They cannot and will not be impounded into such future interpretations unless the reactionary groups or elements will somewhat bow down before the tide of new spiritual knowledge which is to come into the world in a future time. Likewise, the liberal group may learn to develop within its ranks the element of the clairvoyant diagnostician who can properly evaluate and interpret the various psychic structures as they exist in the individual's psychic consciousness. However, dear ones, I see that the Channel is becoming a little distressed, and so we shall discontinue here for the present time.

— Meng Tse.

CHAPTER XC

To my dear brothers and sisters on the earth, I am the personal identity of a former resident of the earth by the name of Emanuel Swedenborg, and lived on the earth world at the time of the Reformation in the 1700's. I must bow first in humble observance, in appreciation, and thanks to the various members of the 'Swedenborg Society' and say in all sincerity and honesty that I thank you from the bottom of my heart for such interests which will further speed and stimulate spiritual progress in the hearts and minds of mankind. My personal earth history relates me in the first fifty years of my life to such dimensions of endeavor as were more or less scientific in the fields of mathematics, physics, mining, and such sundry applications. However, the true dimension of perspective in my servitude to mankind did not come in until I was able to embark into the spiritual dimension of consciousness, and until I had developed a sensitivity with something which might be called a channel of interpretation. A certain mediumistic sense or clairvoyance was attained at that time so that I was enabled to present to the earth some fractions of the spiritual knowledge and spiritual descriptions which were contained in the descriptive literature of the "Seven Celestial Kingdoms".

I would first, before we continue our exploration here, like to somehow enlarge the concepts as they were, in themselves, quite relative to the time and place in which I lived. You will further see that these "Seven Celestial Dimensions or Kingdoms", as I called them, are, in themselves, vast perspectives or dimensions of spiritual knowledge, wisdom, and expression; and from any such individual's concept, it is physically impossible to convey even one small fraction of what is actually in existence. In the beginning of the series of the books of "The Pulse of Creation", it was so conceived in the minds of the more advanced personalities, knowing, as they did, the confines of dimension of thinking within each individual of the earth — and even though they were considered advanced in their time or that they had achieved such academic degrees — yet these factors or relativity were so contained within the dimension in which they were thus living, that no man could supercede the bounds of this dimension, save a medium or a clairvoyant.

The separation of physical flesh is usually, in man's thinking, called death; however, there are many kinds of separation of the physical flesh or the physical minds with the identity of the personality so that one may glimpse portions of the vast and infinite universe about him; and so these Advanced Minds began gradually enlarging their descriptions of the different transmissions, the dimensions of relationship, and adding and increasing the perspective horizon of each individual who so read the lines. Thus, the individual is able to rationalize and to interject into a definite form or concept to a much greater degree, the contents of the transmission. He would not suffer the impact of a sudden revelation which would create a certain type of psychic block within his mind; he would thus be enabled to conceive, and the purpose of the book would not be defeated.

As the planet Venus was related in an astral dimension to the servitude of such terrestrial planets as the earth in the capacity of spiritual therapy and enlightenment, so it developed that the other six centers which have been, and are being revealed to you, are likewise functioning in such dimensional capacities. The central planet Eros is, in itself, somewhat of a dimension and if we can integrate these concepts into something which might be like a link in a chain, the planet Eros, itself, as it was called a planet is actually one of the thirty-three Logi or dimensions as they have been somewhat described to you. Within each of these thirty-three dimensions are such structures similar to that of Eros.

If we can refer temporarily to the original concept of the soap bubble (as in the first chapters of "The Book of Venus") and to the tiny round globules of air, these adhesive molecules of the soap have so related these particles together in somewhat of a linked fashion similar as children would be in the way in which they play in a circular fashion by linking their hands together and dancing around in a circle. Eros, in itself, was portrayed as being several times the size of the earth. However, this was done, not because we did not know any better, or that we were purposely misaligning information to you, or to anything which might be considered unworthy, but the planet Eros, itself, would be of such size, in its own relative capacity, that the earth could be dropped upon the surface of Eros and it would appear about like dropping a pea into a tub of water. Or, the earth, in turn if it were in the same dimension as is Eros, would be similar to dropping a very small pebble into the middle of the large ocean, and this concept might be extended on out into Infinity. The relationship of time and space in the third dimension, is, in itself, one which has puzzled and confounded the most learned savants of the earth, such as Newton and Einstein; they, in themselves very often floundered beyond their depths in the mathematical formulas which superseded the bounds of their finite minds.

To somewhat familiarize you with the concept of time and space, if I can be permitted to do so, we shall begin by saying that an airplane of your time, and day, sitting upon the surface of a landing field, occupies a certain space. This space is, in its present position, immutable. This is because the atoms of energy which constituted the metal are so linked together and extending their energies into such excursions as to become molecular adhesive particles; and this, in turn, fabricated the element known as aluminum, so, thus, the airplane was so constructed and fabricated together that it became a functional unit into the aerobic structures of the atmosphere.

The airplane could sit there from now until it disintegrated into its more earthly elements if it did not have the extra outward motivating force which was interjected into it from the motors. Thus, it was enabled, in the space of a certain length of time, to travel from one city to another. In traveling from these two different points, we can say that the airplane, in its dimension of time, also occupied a much greater dimension of space. We see therefore, the definite linkage of relationship with time and with space. Now, if the atoms in the aluminum could expand simultaneously to occupy a space between the two cities in something like a bridge, this would be annihilating both time and space in the general concept. However, you might think this very impractical in view of the fact that people would have to thus scuttle back and forth like mice or rats across this bridge to go from city to city. This of course would be very unrelative to the rest of the dimension in which these atoms were at that time occupying in attempting to annihilate time and space in a dimension in which they were so conceived.

We would therefore have to continue our hypothetical allegory to entirely include the universe about you. The entire world would thus be expanded, or shall I say, converted into such a condition wherein the atoms, themselves, would all combine and unite with each other so that space and time were thus annihilated, and that any individual would thus be at any time and in any place where he had so conceived without the intercession of outside e.m.f. or electrical motivating force. This is something which may or may not be quite clear to you at this time, but I believe that it will give you some platform or elevation to continue the excursions of mind into some of the factors which are relative to time and space.

The scientist of today conceives, in his own dimension, that all transitions or forms of energy are unrelative or that they may or may not occupy certain boundaries of transmission. Sound too, for instance, can be said to have a mean level of transition of 1,100 feet per second but this depends considerably upon the temperature or the air pressure at the elevation in which the sound is thus being transmitted; also, that certain solids can transmit sound about ten or fifteen times faster than air at any other level of transition. Thus, you see that sound depends entirely upon the conductivity of the substance through which it must transmit itself. Like the stone tossed into the pond making the waves recede to the shore, so the water is said to be the resistive element of transmission. It is both resistive and conductive; so it is with all substances as they are termed elemental or molecular structures in the earth about you.

The scientist, such as Einstein, has conceived the ultimate dimension, and, incidentally, he says that the only single stable form of the transmission of energy is electronic in nature or the speed of light. All electricity and light and the transmission of energy in this spectrum maintains, as he says, the constant relative speed of 186,310 miles per second. We will pause a moment for a further allegory. If we can picture a tiny little ant traveling back and forth across the trails to and from his hill, he will pass numerous grains of sand. To the ant, these grains of sand assume the proportions of large boulders. As the ant is not able, within his capacity of eye structures or sensory capabilities to achieve anything beyond a very limited concept, he cannot look up into the world about him and see things as they are. Nor could he rationalize these things into his concept if he had so conceived them. Let us not misjudge the ant; he is very intelligent in his own little dimension, in his own, shall I say — pardon the word— 'instinctive' reactionary way.

However, man or the savant of today is in much the same position as the ant; and to look up into the dimension about him would necessarily entail the use of the organs of perception to which he has limited himself by saying that he does not have them. He does have these sensory organs within the structures of his mind or his psychic body, but he has ignored them in the great flux of materialism about him.

The ants, the birds, the beasts of the field, in fact even the very plants themselves, all exhibit a comparatively vast amount of this clairvoyance or the linkage to other dimensions of relationship which they have conceived in their own present form or dimension. Man alone, in his own eager and insatiable thirst for things which are relative to his physical nature has not yet conducted himself into these higher dimensions or perspectives of transition. He is so absorbed with what he sees, or senses with his eyes, ears, nose, and what he can taste, or that he can balance himself upon his legs, or that he can move about in the realm and dimension of his senses that he has ignored the greatest part of his whole creation which is his seventh sense. This, in itself, does present somewhat of a strange paradox unless we are completely analytical in our general equations of the position of man in his own particular dimension at that time. It is quite natural for man not to supersede the balance of his consciousness into what he can conceive as emotional experience. The third dimension was contrived by the Infinite Mind of God for such a plane of relative conception and induction of the factors of his everyday evolution into man's mind.

It would not be wise or well to give knowledge beyond the concept of any individual just as we would not give sharp instruments to a child with which to play. A man always has a tendency to use such knowledge or wisdom which is beyond his immediate equation of values in the realm of destructiveness. We have seen this happen so very avidly and portrayed so factually in integrating his knowledge of what he calls his atomic or nuclear science. However, like the small infant who first learns to walk, the first steps are apt to be quite frequently of a very tottering, insecure value of equilibrium; and the child must necessarily plunge, from time to time, upon his face, or thus injure himself and bruise his little body in trying to manipulate his legs before he learns to function in a normal and in an automatic way.

Speaking of paradoxes, you are now seeing about you some rather familiar looking rooms, if we can call these huge dimensions such, wherein you find yourself. They seem to remind you some way of the clinics or hospitals which you may visit from time to time upon your earth, and indeed, these are such healing centers. We are in the section which is directly related to the psychiatric or psychological sciences as they are so propagated at this time within the dimension of man's thinking on the earth. Studying the history of psychology and the treatment of mental aberrations, it was just about fifty years ago when people were confined in cages or in the barred inclosures; they were treated worse than the perverted form of wild animals. They were fed bones, or scraps, or doused with water or left in freezing temperatures without clothing, and all kinds of horrible brutalities were delivered upon them. It was only within the last fifty years or so that the last remnants or wreckages of such treatment among the mentally aberrated were somewhat completely eliminated.

There were many souls or humanitarians who indulged in the liberation of these poor temporarily deranged people. But here again we will say, while the clinic or hospital is a very clean and sanitary place, and these patients are indeed treated in a much more humanitarian way and with consideration, still it is merely one step forward in the general direction. It will take some time before the psychologist will reach the doorway which will conduct him into a new realm or dimension in the treatment of the mentally ill people. This is a strange paradox, incidentally, with the psychiatrist, in the treatment of mentally ill patients, for if you would approach the psychiatrist and even so much as broach the subject of exorcism, or suggest that a person could be obsessed with evil spirits, this doctor would quite likely sneer in your face, or he might laugh out loud, or he may say something very unkind to you. Yet in his treatment for these patients, he is actually conducting a form of exorcism. Whether or not he is aware of it, he is casting out evil spirits in all the forms of therapies which are thus conducted in his own dimension and within his own clinic.

In order to understand this better, we will refer you to some such entity who has entered in, temporarily, and obsessed completely the mind of some patient, and that he is, shall we say, a paranoid or a schizoid. It can be seen that the obsessing entity is, therefore, at least in partial control of the mental faculties of the patient in exhibiting the wild transitions of inharmony and inclusions about him. So, the patient is strapped in a chair or bed, electrodes placed on the forehead, and electricity is applied. The shock and the pain is immediately felt by the obsessing entity. It is like sticking a long sharp knife in the posterior anatomy of a human being, and the entity will recoil in just the same such manner. He will jump back and tear himself loose from the individual, and the individual will be thus temporarily freed from this obsessing influence. However, it does not mean a cure because just as soon as the shock is removed, the entity is quite likely to come back and occupy his former position.

Any practitioner can tell you that in advanced cases the continual shock treatments do absolutely no good except in temporary forms of relief. This is because the obsessing entity is now so thoroughly attached to the individual's psychic body, that it cannot be dislodged even by large applications of pain in the form of shock. Other forms of shock are introduced into the patient such as playing icy streams of water from a hose upon him; or, in some instances, other brutalities are expressed, and I mean that all of these forms are brutal in nature. While it is said that the patient does not suffer from shock treatment, yet he does suffer and so does the entity. In the form of the water treatment, here again the obsessing entity is plunged into some fearful sense of drowning so that he quickly leaves the poor individual temporarily, at least for a little while.

To extend the concepts of obsession just a little further as to how these obsessing entities are incurred, we will say that in most cases entities are, in themselves, individuals who have become quite perverted in their attitudes and respect toward the general way of life as man exists; they are more or less similarly earth bound in their own equation or value of position. They will thus hang around old buildings or old houses which are reminiscent or familiar to the way in which they formerly lived upon the earth. A person who lives in such a building is quite likely to become partially obsessed and can easily take on physical or mental forms of illness or aberrations simply because the person is ignorant of these obsessing entities which are clustered about the house and within its vibration. These obsessing entities do not necessarily need to be people; they can be, and frequently are the thought form bodies which have lived or have been projected as murderous forms into the rooms of the buildings;

thus they become apparitions or spirits which are seen from time to time. If the persons who live in such buildings are not properly protected, and do not realize what is happening about them, they can quite easily become obsessed.

A woman who has died of cancer in such a building can, in that fear and in the consequence of that fear, and dying as she did in that malformed condition of pain and psychic impact, so relive her experience for many, many years in that same old building. Moreover, any other person who comes into that building may be immediately seized upon by that obsessing entity as a haven of temporary refuge, or that she may feel in the vibration of this human contact some warmth or some strength, or some sense of familiarity; so that in due course of time, this person who has been entered into can, and frequently does, incur the cancerous condition in exactly the same place as it was incurred in the former inmate of the house.

So the problem with the psychiatrist who treats such a person or that the doctor may say, "Well, you have a cancer, you must be operated on," is not, in any sense of the word, freeing the individual from the cancer if it is removed from the portion of the physical body; so the obsessing entity then again enters in and the cancer is continued into further excursions about the body. Cancer, as you know, is merely the indisposition or the misalignment of energy entering into certain atomic structures in the body. The atoms have lost their proper spiritual guidance, their direction or support from the higher spiritual planes, and from such constituting and supporting vortices of energy in the atomic structures, the atom becomes unrelevant, or it speeds up its negative course in such a wild and frantic way that it becomes malignant and spreads its cancerous or malignant or speeded up nature into other atomic structures near it. The mere operation and removal of a malignant tumor from a person's body does not mean that he is cured from cancer. Every doctor knows that following through the lymphatic tissues of the human body, the murderous or maligned atoms of energy, in various molecular structures, can re-enter and further propagate their wild and murderous intent into other structures of the body.

In a general conclusion we can say that the present doctor or psychiatrist or psychologist, in whatever type or psychoanalysis or therapy in which he is so engaged, is still comparatively in the dark ages of his transition, even though he may pride himself with his laboratory, his operating rooms, or his various types of apparatus; yet these types of therapy, in themselves, are comparatively primitive, for he is still essentially dealing with nothing more or less than some of the more reactionary concepts of psychoanalysis as they were conceived in the more primitive expressions of exorcism which are practiced in the more primitive tribes of mankind on the earth today. The witch doctor in the jungle who beats upon drums, dresses himself in a fearsome mask and garb, and dances about a sick person is trying to scare out the entity. The modern practitioner, psychiatrist or psychologist, in clamping the electrodes on the forehead of the individual is also scaring out the entity. There is no difference except in the way in which this exorcism is practiced. We can say, in general conclusion, therefore, that the witch doctor is a little more intelligent in his expression, because he realizes that it is an obsessing entity which has made the person ill, whereas the psychiatrist does not recognize such a thing as an evil spirit. He can, therefore, be said to be less intelligent than the savage.

Now I know that these words will quite likely create some rather harsh reactions in the minds of some of the scientists of the world who may read these lines in the future; but I do say this to you in all sincerity, that as you are all brothers and sisters and that you have love and the understanding of the humanitarian aspects in the treatment of your fellow man in such diseased portions of his mind or anatomy; and as we are universally, one and all, interested in the betterment of mankind, we will put aside the emotional or the temporal reactions of our minds and induct into ourselves the proper concepts in the manner in which intelligent human beings are supposed to be conducive in their evaluations of concepts between one another. We shall do this on the grounds that, as we are intelligent human beings, and that we may or may not have incurred such predispositions, or such boundaries, or circumscribed limits within the dimension of our own minds, that it is not necessarily so that we should always adhere to the certain circumscribed lines of demarcation.

This is entirely unintelligent, and the true scientist or doctor is always seeking a new avenue, a new horizon and a new expression. The mere fact in the interpretations of the psychiatric versions of therapies as they are produced in the world today, and in the high rate of incidence of mental illness as it is portrayed throughout the cities of your civilization, shows that you are indeed very badly and very sadly in need of a new horizon and a new dimension in which you can exercise the instinctive humanitarian expressions of your own nature.

To cure or heal people in whatever way or capacity you are able, means that you are going to have to raise or expand your perspective or horizon beyond the dimension in which it is now contained. We do not mean that you must revert back to the primitive expression of the savage as he expressed exorcism or witchcraft in the jungle. There is indeed a much higher and more advanced type of therapy which is entirely scientific in its nature and is reproductive of entirely one hundred per

989

cent results in positive cures which can reinstate a person back into a functional dimensional relationship with his fellow man.

So in conclusion, my dear brothers and sisters, and to my fellow practitioners or scientists, in whatever dimension you are thus expressing yourselves, seek earnestly. Do not condemn or criticize, for there is truth to be found in even the lowest and more elemental forms of human expression upon the earth today. Do not think that you have arrived at any state of perfection or that you have even achieved a borderline of such advancement, but you must know that the future days will hold wonderful and great revelations of truths to the races of mankind. Until such time, to my dear ones and to my brothers and sisters, this has been a great privilege accorded to me; your most humble servant.

— Swedenborg.

Again from Helianthus: I am the identity of Louis Pasteur, the Frenchman who lived in the 1800's (1822-1895), and was associated with the field of science in the exploration of what is called the science of bacteriology and antiseptics. As everyone knows, the word or name 'Pasteur' means pasteurization of milk, and even the high school student knows that I was associated, somewhat, with the developing of certain processes or techniques in the science of bacteriology in producing the various antibiotic agents, such as immunization of sheep against anthrax and worked with the anti-rabies serums. I would like to point out, at this time, that a great deal of false emphasis or credence is given to the word 'discovery'. A man never discovers anything; he is, in his daily process of life — in whatever plane he finds himself — merely tuning back into the dimension of his higher self, so that he will automatically conceive within his physical or material mind, some elements of truth or concept with which he has previously been in very close contact. The mere act of discovering some scientific truth or some such concept as is commonly associated with the word discovery, invention, or such kindred concepts of mind are, an intuition, merely an actual flash of integration in which the individual is materializing into his dimension of concept on the earth, as he so exists, this previously interrelated concept wherein he has studied, or so been instructed in this particular concept in a higher dimension or a different realm.

The act of evolution on the earth is, in itself, an act of metamorphosis or a cycle which is quite similar, in many respects, to that which other worlds and other terrestrial planets have gone through, or are going through in our present day and age. It can, likewise, be assumed that such further cyclic evolutions will continue, not only for your own planet, but for the many other and innumerable planets which exist in the great so-called voids of space.

Now, I would like to talk further about some of these facets of life which you find about you, for we believe that in introspection, the individual can arrive at some point in his personal philosophy which will, to a degree, immunize him against the psychic impacts or the different interpolations of life which exist about him in his present reincarnation upon the earth. We have pointed out the oppressive sense of consciousness which has been developed from the superabundance of laws in their various and numerous interpolations, and in the bureaucracies which exist in the governmental systems; and that individuals are, in a sense of the word, becoming very fearsome. They seem to think that these laws are like some huge juggernaut which is poised above them and ready to fall upon and crush them at any time.

It is in a revolt against these fears that the average child learns to steal or to rebel against the confines and restricted impact of the psychic nature of these systems of social structures in which he has found himself. These first propensities of rebellion which will later develop into criminal characteristics are, sometimes, very strongly fortified with some previous reincarnation wherein the individual may have committed more or less, some type of a felony or may have been a law-breaker. The whole idea or concept of law, as it has existed in the pages of history in the numerous nations and civilizations, is one which is primarily concerned with punishing the person after he has committed the crime.

In posing the question of law, it is merely supposed that in the fear of some aspect of a natural consequence of judgment, a person may be deterred from such acts which would precipitate some judgment upon him. This concept is, in itself, as fallacious as many of the other concepts which man has derived from a reactionary way of life. If as much effort, time, and money were spent in proper education and into proper alignment procedures into the life of the newly born child as he develops into the state of adulthood, there would be far less of the criminal nature manifested in the social structures of your time and place. The penal institutions are but a step removed from the dungeons of medieval times. The modern penitentiary, is in itself, a huge and somewhat modern institution that contains plumbing and electricity, and there are numerous other conditions which are considered modern; yet the very idea of incarceration to the criminal is just as oppressive as in the days when he was thrown into a dark dungeon and was forced to sleep upon a bed of vermin-infested straw. Here, again, is the principle of revolt. It is in this rebellion of mind against these structures which, roughly creates the most corrupt and vilest passions of man's nature. The prevention or circumvention of such passions in any individual's nature is of the utmost importance in relieving him of such stresses in his daily life which are inductive to the numerous psychic derelictions of anger, rebellion, and hatred, or to the more insidious poison of fear.

As we have seen in the fields of medicine or psychiatry that here again man has not truly integrated himself with his spiritual nature and dimension of things about him. Until such a time wherein such things can take place, man will continue in more or less of the same reactionary pattern of life. Ignorance breeds fear, and in the misunderstanding and misconceptions of the true nature and purpose of the inner self of man, this ignorance itself creates these numerous derelictions of expression in the physical structures, which are in some relative dimension of expression in which the individual so finds himself.

Getting back to my original topic, for I have strayed somewhat from my original intent and purpose, I would like to discuss some of the still practiced and so-called 'modern concepts' of antiseptics, or the relative impacts into what I would like to call the dairy industry and into the consumption of the numerous dairy products as they so exist in your present social structure. There is, at your present time, a large amount of propaganda which is being circulated as to the value of drinking large quantities of milk. As a whole, the dairy industry in your country can be said to be one which is very highly exploited, and is, in itself, a very vast industry upon which many people depend for their very living. I would not, in any sense of the word, tend to arouse any antagonism in the minds of any individuals who are connected with the dairy industry, or to the different companies which are so employed in distributing and selling the milk products as they are found in your numerous cities.

The process of pasteurization, as everyone knows, merely means that in raising the temperature of the milk to the point of about 65 degrees centigrade, most of the bacteria which may be found in that milk will be destroyed. This must be followed by an immediate cooling process. The pasteurization, as it was so founded and conceived in my time, was merely a stop-gap measure. It must be remembered that in those days sanitation or septics was comparatively unknown. People had little or no knowledge about bacteria, and the average individual or anyone who was engaged in producing milk or any dairy product was totally unaware of the various sources of contamination which might have entered into the production of that milk. It was therefore found that many diseases were spread by drinking milk, and an effort was made to stop that contamination. A farmer who produced milk in those days merely did so by sitting down in the barnyard, or in the barn with a pail between his knees, and sitting upon a three-legged stool, proceeded to relieve the cow of her burden of milk. The idea that dust or germs could fall into the milk while he was milking did not enter the farmer's head, or that he was emptying the cow's udder into a contaminated pail, was likewise far removed from his consciousness. He may have set the half-opened pail in a nearby stream of running water to cool it, or he may have put it in the milk house until he could further go about the process of distribution or remanufacture this milk into butter or some other dairy product. Into whatever field this milk was diverted, however, the same lack of understanding of contamination was further manifest. So, as a consequence, milk very often reached the consumer, either in one way or another, in different forms, as a very highly contaminated source of food; and, as a consequence, epidemics and plagues were sometimes literally induced by the distribution of milk from one particular farmer, or from one certain cow.

As everyone should know, the cow herself is a carrier of a large number of disease germs just as is a human. It can be found that cows are contaminated through their associations with humans; they may incur very large indispositions of tubercular bacillus, or the tubercular germ. A person who drinks or uses dairy products which are contaminated with the tubercle bacilli will soon grow the nodules of the germ along the intestinal tract, and the germs may break loose in his blood stream and reinfect different portions of his body. These are facts which must be entered into in the relations and consumption of milk. Nor is tubercle bacillus the only contaminating germ which is dangerous to humans; we find also that people can incur undulant fever from drinking milk from infected cows. This is a virus condition which produces a tremendously high rate of fever which is usually fatal to humans. The cow may or may not have undulant fever, but can still carry the virus in her system.

Now, let us consider the necessity of drinking milk and, as I have somewhat hinted, there has been a great deal of false emphasis placed on milk and its relative value as a food in your present civilization. Examining the numerous races of mankind upon the terrestrial earth, we find that the Eskimo would not know what milk is, as it is produced in the dairies of your centers of civilization. An Eskimo baby being born into the world is, within a few days time, chewing upon a piece of blubber, so that within two or three months he is completely weaned. A Polynesian mother will start, within two or three days, to feed a child the pulp of a mashed banana, and in the course of a month or so, the child is largely sub-existing on fruit. You have seen African pictures wherein the natives carried their babies upon their backs in some sort of sack or pouch, and they would swing the babies around under their arms and nurse them at their breasts. This, too, is done strictly from necessity. In Africa if you were to feed a baby on bottled milk, he would quite likely very quickly die unless the milk was continually purified by sterilization. The nipple merely forms a convenient method of permitting the baby to take nourishment into his body in a strictly uncontaminated way; nor can the mother lay the child down upon the grass or other places, as some prowling beast or some vermin might come up and carry off or bite the child and it would be destroyed.

The women in your modern world and in your time today are too concerned with the many and various duties around the household, or the activities of various clubs and social functions to be burdened, or to be encumbered with the nursing of their children, so they have found a very convenient method of merely placing the baby on a bottle formula. Bottle nursing will be considered somewhat further along in my discussion, but let us continue in what I call consumption of milk as it is found in the numerous races and tribes of peoples of the world.

In Tibet the people of that country usually use the milk of the yak. A yak can be said to be something quite similar to a long-haired cow. Yak milk in Tibet is nearly always processed before it is consumed as raw milk, and is considered somewhat inedible in such a raw state. A native of Tibet will coagulate or process this milk into some form of cheese, or he may use the butter in his tea; however, in all cases the milk is first broken down chemically by the natural processes which are involved in fermentation or the bacteria of the acidophilus, introducing lactic acid within the milk which tends to break down the protein constituents of milk into some form of a curd structure.

In Arabia, milk in its raw state is largely goat's milk which, incidentally, is largely much more palatable and more easily digested than cow's milk. Goat's milk is naturally homogenized, and the cream never rises in a vessel of goat's milk. It is also much richer and more readily assimilated into the human system than cow's milk. An Arab will pour his goat milk into the dried stomach of a goat, or into some suitable bag made of a hide or skin and sling it over the back of his camel and ride through the desert sun until the milk has been reduced into some form of cottage cheese by fermentation in the hot desert sun. This then, is considered palatable to the Arabian, as the milk is now comparatively predigested.

One sees a youngster, in a mad haste, dash from school into one of your modern homes. His mother will immediately place into his hands a large glass of ice-cold homogenized and pasteurized milk from the refrigerator, which the child, in haste, gulps down in one long draft. The mother thinks she is doing something very good for the child but this, in itself, creates a tremendous disturbance in the child's stomach. The child cannot digest the milk in that state, and it must, upon meeting hydrochloric acid in the stomach, be converted or reduced to small shred-like curds before it can be suitably broken down by further reactions of the gastric juices of the stomach. When milk is converted to numerous types of cottage cheese or into other types of cheese, it becomes a predigested food inasmuch as the protein structures of milk are broken down and reduced into a palatable and digestible form before being taken into the stomach and intestinal tract. I would say to you mothers, that if you must give your child milk, and as it is always obtained in the markets as pasteurized milk, that it should be first slightly warmed and the child should drink it through some of the straws which are found in the soda fountains or the drug stores. A very slow sipping of this milk will be of much greater value in the process of assimilation and digestion in the child's stomach.

Going further along into the line of thinking, into the inception of lactose or into the period of nursing and to the common practice of putting the baby upon a bottle formula, let us first go into what we call the psychic nature of the individuals of the mother and the child in their relationship. It has largely been pointed out that the relationship of love, and to such similar attachments in family homes, as they are called love or family or domestic ties are purely the product of vibration as they exist in the psychic consciousness of each individual in his relationship to the various members of the family about him. The harmonious or compatible rates of vibration as they are mingling in a psychic nature with each other, are the greatest and the more purely refined concepts of this love. These harmonic structures can, of course, extend on up into the very highly developed superconsciousness of the individual. These facts must be remembered when we are dealing with the problem of bringing a child into the world and seeing that he is properly started upon the path of life.

At the moment of conception there is an inception of the psychic body of the soon-to-be child within the psychic domain of the mother. The strong attachment, as

I have pointed out, is in the expression of frequency relationships, and that they are now actually related to each other, at the moment of conception, in a psychic way. A doctor can point out to you that there is actually no nerve interconnection between the newly conceived fetus and the mother; however, he has sadly neglected the factor of psychic relationship. As it begins to grow in the womb of the mother, the newly conceived child is in direct psychic contact with the mother at all times. Through this reaction of osmosis and through the placenta and the umbilical cord, are contained the constituents of blood and the transfusion of energy and such other substances which are necessary to build the child's body. There is also the psychic interchange between the child and the mother. The child may not have the mental reactive mechanism known as brain structures or the brain as it is known in your time; however, he does have a beginning of a brain, but it is still an instrument to be developed by the ordinary emotional processes of life. Within the child's psychic body and within the mother's psychic body there is a definite interchange; the child may have been previously associated with the mother in a former life, or in some cases is an entirely newly conceived contact which is brought into relationship through the same laws and orders of harmonic structures. Very often the biune or the soul mate of the mother will enter the world through her womb. Usually, in the case of families of three or four or more, the last child born into the world by the mother is her biune or soul mate.

Now, we have established somewhat, the psychic relationship of the child with the mother. This, therefore, is the period of gestation and is a cycle. The second cycle which the child enters into is the cycle of lactation. This more properly means that the child should immediately enter into the process of nursing the mother's breast. The first nursing consists of a sort of fluid that enters the child's stomach, which produces an action which is mostly purgative in nature and physics the child, freeing the intestinal tract of such impediments as have been formed by lack of peristalsis in the child's intestinal tract in the function of digestion, which as yet has not been properly entered into. This fluid of the first nursing immediately creates, stimulates, and brings into life the necessary peristalsis, the functions of the intestinal tract. After several repeated nursings, the milk emerges from the various glands which are associated with the breast structure. Here the child enters into a new psychic relationship with the mother and which is of the utmost importance to him in his future life.

Here he begins to lay down the very foundation of his whole future, in terms of the personal sense of security. It is in any of the violations of this personal sense of security that the child may suffer impingements or neurotic indispositions which will be very psychosomatic in nature. Before I proceed, however, I would like to point out that in the period of gestation there are also other dangers which I neglected to mention. These are what I call poisons through the blood stream and presented to the child through osmotic function of interchange. A mother who smokes is inducing into her blood stream great quantities of carbon monoxide and other coal tar derivatives, which are poisonous in nature; and these will eventually find their way into the body of the fetus within the womb. A mother who smokes or indulges in mental disturbances, such as anger, hatred, or resentment, will, in direct proportion, incept into the child's body the numerous poisons which these things, all in themselves, produce. Therefore, the woman who is to become a mother must remember that from the point of conception on, she must maintain a very complacent mental attitude. The mental health of her own self is of the utmost importance in the future relationship to the child. In five minutes of anger a woman can generate enough poison in her body to actually kill a small dog. This has been proven. This poison could be incepted into the fetus of the child and produce great harm in the body structures of the child. In fact, in some cases it can even cause a premature abortion!

The continual inhalation of cigarette smoke precipitates a great quantity of carbon monoxide into the blood stream. This is a deadly poison and one, in itself, which has a very damaging effect, especially into the circulatory system of the fetus of the child. This child is quite likely, in his future evolutions of life, to suffer pulmonary disturbances of the lungs, or that he may suffer such malformations as arteriosclerosis, hypertension, or breaking down of the natural functions of the heart itself. Your science of today has only partially succeeded in demonstrating the relationship of cigarette smoking with lung cancer or lip cancer; also, associated with such practices of smoking we can relate hardening of the arteries and various other malfunctions of the human system.

The ramifications of this understanding cannot be over-emphasized, and in the future days of science — when they have disassociated themselves from the aspect of fear and from the commercial systems as they exist in your time and place — they can fully explain to the general public the pernicious effect of cigarette smoking on the human system. At present the tobacco companies are huge cartels which are highly organized and are exploiting the public to the fullest extent and dominion of what is defined as the democratic system. Under this democratic system you can easily see that such exploitations are in direct contradiction to an intelligent interaction between personal analyses and the evaluation of such falsely superimposed structures which may exist in your social system. The mere fact that a company can exploit or sell its product does not, in any sense of the word, mean that it is good for you.

1001

This is the threshold of your own personal self-analysis, and one in which you must properly evaluate everything — not only that which goes into your body, but also that which goes into your mind.

Now that we have considered somewhat the period of gestation in the child and how the various poisons and such disturbances which arise within the daily practice of the mother's life can be very serious, future impediments in the normal, natural, physical and mental functions of the future child, so can the period of lactation be equally or even more important to the future development of the child. Usually, a mother who nurses her child upon the breast, does so until some such period of time that she believes he can be weaned; then suddenly the breast is taken away from the child and he is forced into eating a more semi-solid diet. This weaning, creates a tremendous psychic impact into the nature of the child; for, all of a sudden, he is deprived of that personal sense or touch of security. If the mother had followed a general line of practice, as it is exhibited among the so-called primitive races of the earth in starting to wean the child within a few days at the time of birth, the child would not suffer this great psychic impact of his loss of the sense of security. He would naturally develop a liking for the semi-solid or the solid diet which would enable him to desist from the breast nursing.

A woman who places her child upon the bottle immediately after birth, not only deprives herself of one of the greatest joys of motherhood, which is suckling the babe upon her breast, but she also deprives the babe of his first and greatest relationship to the new world in which he finds himself. He is automatically, to a large extent, displaced in his relationship; he does not know the love and the tenderness, and the association which is found in nursing the nipple of his mother's breast. Here, in the mingling of the function of nursing is the actual building and mingling of the child's dimension of relationship which will enable him to progress further into the world about him. You can easily see that if he is deprived of that first natural relationship, he will, in direct proportion, suffer to a considerable extent. In what has been called the psychosomatic concept of the psychiatrist of today, he will tell you this is the most formative, and incidentally, the place in a child's life where he incurs the greatest indispositions of reflexes; these can become the neurotic thought patterns of his future life.

The fallacious folly of bottle feeding can also be enlarged upon in that the child is drinking a processed milk. This milk, as always, has already been sterilized, or it has been pasteurized so that such forms of bacteria existing in the milk are largely disposed of. It has not ocurred to the doctor or to the mother that in partial cooking of the milk only a portion of the protein structures of the milk are partially altered and that milk is largely a protein structure, or that it is more commonly known as casein.

The chemist of your day can produce a very good quality of adhesive or glue from this casein. If casein is not properly broken down before it enters the body it is quite natural that the body has to do this breaking down process. It is more logical to break down this milk before it enters the body, or that it is at least in a form that can be more readily broken down. In the process of pasteurization, only a partial change has been brought about with the process of heat. The protein structures are so altered as to make them almost totally indigestible. A child fortunately nurses the milk rather warm, and as it goes through the small hole of the nipple into his stomach, such curds as are produced with the contact of the acids of the gastric juice are largely in a digestible form; however, the milk from the breast of the mother is one which is directly related to the time and dimension of the child's own nature. It is not only a material milk, but in a sense of the word is also a psychic milk. A cow is an animal and is not related psychically to a child in any sense of the word. Even the milk of the goat is much more easily digested in the stomach of the child than the milk of a cow.

In many parts of the world the first food an infant eats after only a few days, and in many instances within only a few minutes after his birth, is a curd which is a form of cottage cheese. As I have said, the process of pasteurization, as was brought into the world at my time and in my work on the earth was merely a stop-gap measure; it was the lesser of two evils. It did remove some contamination from milk and in the process of removing this contamination, it also destroyed large numbers of the bacteria which were necessary in breaking down the protein structures of the milk. These acidophilus bacteria are very necessary to any person who drinks milk; they should be in large numbers in the milk before it is taken into the stomach, and that future digestion of milk depends largely on the content of acidophilus organisms in the milk itself. The destruction of this germ in making the milk completely sterile is further impeding the natural digestive processes of the human system.

We surely need not mention the important factor, which any high school student should know, in regard to the changing of vitamin and mineral content by heat, as extreme temperature in either direction changes a certain amount of nutritional value so far as bodily benefit is concerned. Also, some milk is being artificially vitamin-plussed, or synthetic vitamins are being added after the pasteurization. However, the amount of vitamins which are being added per unit (quart) is far insufficient to compensate for the destruction of the natural ones along with the fact that synthetic vitamins do not compare in true value or benefit to the natural ones. We here in these Centers can see, in the future, what the impact will be if the mothers of the civilized world continue in the practice of bottle feeding the babies with cow's milk. It is a fact that infants only a few weeks old can, and sometimes do, as every doctor knows — begin to develop peptic or duodenal ulcers; these ulcers, generally, are products of emotional insecurity which have been developed because the child does not know the security of the mother's breast.

We can link other childhood diseases which are considered incurable. Doctors do not know anything about how they are brought about, or the nature of their true origin. We might point out that diabetes, properly, is a disturbance of the ductless glands of the body which is produced as a direct reflex from this sense of insecurity in the child. The psychiatrist and doctor know that in diabetes there is a strong linkage in the emotional nature of the child, and if a child is diabetic in nature, he is emotionally indisposed in some way; he has a neurosis, and very often this diabetic child has peptic or duodenal ulcers. The relationship here will most always be that this child is a bottle fed baby, or that even if he is breast fed, the mother is an extremely neurotic or very nervous type person. Here again is the linkage or the relationship of the psychic nature of the child with that of the mother. The mother or the father is very strongly related in the proper proportions of this psychic relationship in the dimension of the child's newly born interpolation of the world about him. He sees in his mother and father the first apex or affinity of the world about him, his home or the nursery where he is in his first dimension.

Also, from his psychic self, come other impingements of consciousness sometimes called instinct or emotional reflexes which have somewhat puzzled the child psychologist. These emotionalisms, as we have previously explained, are related to previous lives and to conceptions of integration into such previous lives; so all in all, it can be roughly summed up, that the most natural processes of bringing a child into the world should be in effect and his chances for a normal and happy life will be further enhanced if the child is breast fed.

The women of your time and age are rapidly developing breasts which are incapable of supporting the lactic period of a child's life, and nature usually removes or dissolves any part of the human body which is not used in the process of evolution. The scientist might point out that man lost his tail when he began sitting about in chairs and in the various other things of the material world. However, we have pointed out that there is a definite line of demarcation in the evolution of mankind from the animal to the state of homosapiens. It must always be remembered, just as we have so continually and thoroughly emphasized, that man must begin to include in his numerous philosophies and interpolations of science on the earth, the correct and related facets of the psychic dimension of the world about him whether it is in physics, medicine, philosophy, or religion. To properly understand man's true nature and his inward or psychic self is of the utmost importance and when you achieve this understanding, it will be the greatest step you have ever made in the progression of your civilization in any time and in any place.

The future of the world history depends to a large degree upon the immediate future as to the breaking down of sectional bonds of races and creeds and upon relating man to himself in whatever dimension he finds himself in his expression into the universal brotherhood or the free masonry of the new world as it will be conceived in a future evolution. Because he is Hindu, Jew, Arab, American, English, or any other of the races or nationalities on the earth, does not mean that he is, in any sense of the word, different from anyone else. Every man and every individual is constituted with the same body, with the same elements in that body; he has the same psychic structures which are the linkage and relationship with his superconscious self. He is at that present moment, at that stage, going through some phase of his own personal evolution. A correct understanding of the proper relationship of man to himself, the existence of the numerous races and countries of peoples on the earth will, therefore, automatically remove the barriers of the political and ecclesiastical systems which have given rise to the internal wars and strifes of the numerous nations. It is important to properly understand man in his true concept of brotherly love and free masonry. Every individual is entitled to his own place in his evolution; that we can only assist and help him, but at no time should we ever become a person who is destructive or that we have a better way of life than his, and that we would like to show him that our way is better.

His way is better than yours for his own purpose and in his own time. He can never achieve truth until he has properly inter-related himself through the processes of experience in his own dimension. That is the prime and motivating concept behind the evolution of man in relationship to creating for himself some of the abstract nature of infinity. So, continue on in your purpose; continue to push aside the barriers of disillusion of material aspect. I would say to the scientist and the doctor of the world that, as he exists today in his time and dimension, he is to be very highly commended as to what work has been done since my leaving the earth sixty years ago. Tremendous strides have indeed been made in helping to relieve man from some of the material conditions with which he has been so plagued from the beginning of time. As it can be seen, that with the further realization of civilization into new ages and into new dimensions, it can be easily visualized that these dimensions or these new ages and civilizations will likewise bring in their new plagues, their new diseases and new types of mental conditions. Therefore, there must be new sciences, new methods of combatting these destructive elements in man's evolution.

Just as in the various types of sciences as they exist today, certain immunities of organic species can be brought about very quickly during different periods of evolution. A fly can develop, in three or four generations, an immunity to the compound of DDT, so that various other organisms or bacteria can, in a few generations, develop a great immunity to penicillin and other antibiotic drugs; so you will find, as you develop new techniques of killing out these killers, as they exist in TB and other conditions that, genetically, they will soon regenerate into different species which are immune to these antibiotics.

In the future, just as men on other planets have learned to do, you will learn, that through the proper distribution of the psychic intelligence and the psychic energies from other dimensions into the body itself will be the greatest destroyer of these different diseased conditions. Tuberculosis and the healing of TB, as it exists within the human system, can be very quickly and easily eradicated if the individual is properly connected to the healing forces within his psychic nature. No germ or destructive organism can live in the human body if these psychic powers of healing are properly related into the body at a proper time. Nor can other so-called incurable indispositions such as multiple sclerosis, muscular dystrophy, epilepsy, diabetes, high blood pressure, heart conditions of numerous types and kinds exist. They will all be dissipated in the future day when mankind begins to learn to use the great creative forces of his psychic nature within himself.

By abstaining from the reactionary thought processes of negativity, and accepting the sequence of things as they react or seem to press in upon your own dimension, at your own time in your own relationship, you will learn to see that these things are only attracted into your consciousness through the reactionary processes of negativity; and by the reversal of this process, and in the realization that there is a proper sequence of law, order, and harmony expressed into your mind and into your daily way of life, so the more positive expressions too, will not only be reflected into your daily life, but they will also be reflected into your body; your body will develop a great immunity against these conditions which are plaguing mankind. These truths can be further extended into the concept or the dimension of mind where they will become very inhibitive factors which will relieve man of the great burden of inceptive psychological disturbances which have developed into a great strain or path of neurotic indisposition into the face of mankind today.

It has been pointed out that civilization is very conclusive and very productive in its numerous and multiple expressions, in the fears and inhibitions, and in the reflexes which are a daily part and occurrence of the average individual. In these multiplicities and multiplexities of his existence, he very quickly enlarges and strengthens the psychosomatic reflexes and indispositions of his early childhood. He therefore can very quickly come to the time and place where not only his body suffers from the numerous indispositions of some of the incurable diseases, but also, the balance of the body, its endocrine or ductless glandular system is very seriously disturbed, and disturbing this distribution of the essences of hormones in their alchemy of the body, he very quickly falls by the wayside.

The same process is quite true in his mental aspect of life. It is only in familiarizing yourself with the numerous and fearful indispositions of life about you, that you can somehow immunize yourself against them. In the light of proper truth and relationship, you will build about you a certain wall of fortification or immunization. You will also bring into your consciousness higher and more relative factors of dimensional expression which will enable you to incept a vast amount of this psychic energy into your nature, and thus heal yourself from the many multiplicities of these deleterious expressions in your material world about you. I do hope I have not overstayed my time.

— Louie.

P.S. Just as was pointed out, during the period of gestation, toxemia was a very definite possibility in the fetus and that psychic reflexes were also impounded into the nature of the child. It should be emphasized, too, that in the period of lactation or nursing a child, too, can suffer from toxemia which is incepted into the body of the mother. If a mother smokes, a child can suffer a great deal of this type of toxemia; or if the mother is emotionally disturbed, the child too, can suffer. It is quite possible for a mother to take certain drugs or purgatives and induce a similar condition in the child through the process of lactation. In all cases, however, these things in their true relationship must be borne in mind as to whether you determine to bottle nurse or breast feed your baby. To the future women of the world, and particularly to those in America where bottle feeding is of such universal use, women's breasts will largely disappear in coming evolutions; and as I have said, will disappear because they are no longer needed. Remember, also, that in any foods and in your usage of foods, whether they are in relationship to nursing of the baby, or into such usage of life, that if they are synthesized or they have come in contact with metallic pipes or objects of such similar nature, they may have suffered some sort of psychic impingement or relationship to an inorganic substance. These elements such as foods being processed and placed in metal containers will destroy a great deal of the natural psychic relationship of these foods with their true inner nature of the nutritional value as they are so contained in their normal state. If you could eat the fruits and foods directly from the trees and garden, you would be much healthier physically and mentally; but these things are all by-products of the civilization in which you live. The highly developed and synthesized world is productive of numerous physical and mental illnesses, and you should always strive to live as naturally and normally and as complacently as possible.

The thought has occurred to me, while we were on the subject of germs or bacteriology and, as this was the greatest interest of my life while on the earth, that you, too, might find a large amount of introspection in seeing the Infinite Mind of God working in the proper sequence of order and balance in the world about you if I could explain to you, something more of the wonderful and infinite nature of this expression in the microscopic domain. I am presenting these facts to you, not because I wish you to become germ conscious, but that perhaps in these qualities of introspection you can become a better and more well-ordered individual.

A human being is a very arsenal of germs and bacteria. A baby has been found to have, within an hour after birth, at least forty or fifty pathogenic organisms in its mouth. It is common knowledge that the most destructive killers are sometimes the bacteria or the protozoans which infest the bodies of man; they are, also, the most beneficent forms of such plant and animal growth found in these microscopic dimensions. Mankind could not live upon the earth if it were not for bacteria and such micro-organisms, not only around him in the various factors of relationship in removing or refining

1011

different foodstuffs, or in the nature and evolution of all things about him, but that within his and within your own body there are many organisms in the intestinal tract which are called bacteria or algae and, respectively, are all very relative and necessary for you to assimilate your food.

The mere fact that you are a human being does not make you immune from the same type of body functions as are portrayed in the animal life about you. Within the blood stream of every animal is found certain organisms or bacteria. Leucocytes or the phagocytes in the white blood cells of the body are the scavengers, and are waging an unending battle against the invasions of these micro-organisms which have invaded the body, either through inhalation, or through punctures of the skin, or through different invasions from the gastrointestinal tract. The processes of breaking down food such as the protein structures contained in milk and numerous other foods, must first be entered into from the realm of these micro-organisms which are called the lactic acid bacillus. In all milk, including mother's milk, are found large quantities of these acid-forming bacteria which have, even as the child suckles the nipple, already begun to break down the protein structures of the milk so that the child can further assimilate them in the process of digestion. After the milk goes into the stomach, the hydrochloric acid will curdle it into small curds. This is further acted upon by the peptone as the gastric juice is composed of a dozen or more compound acids and peptones. After it leaves the stomach and enters the small intestine, it meets a further digestive process, as there are numerous flagella, or tiny little sponge-like growths growing upon the intestinal wall. In the interstices of these flagella there are small rod-like extrusions of the intestinal wall in which grow the billions and billions of tiny bacteria of different kinds. They can manifest themselves into substance which looks a great deal like the moss upon the stone in a stream. The milk is therefore acted and reacted upon until these elements are broken down into a form which can be assimilated into the lymphatic system of the intestinal walls through the process of induction known as osmosis, or the interchange of food between a membranous tissue.

As every farmer knows, even in a sterilized milking machine, the milk must be immediately removed and cooled in a comparatively low degree temperature, otherwise the milk will begin to spoil. No amount of sterilization of pipes or vessels will exclude this early fermentation in milk as it comes from within the organism of lactic acid; acidophilus bacteria comes from within the cow, herself, just as the same organism comes from within the mother's milk. The problem here in antisepsis is that of excluding the destructive micro-organisms such as the tubercle bacillus, or typhoid bacillus, or various other types of pathogenic organisms and not destroying the necessary acidophilus.

Generally speaking, and according to the accepted public health standards, as they exist in the numerous cities, pasteurization removes all bacterial growth organisms down to a point of about 25,000 per cubic centimeter. This is still a relatively high content of germ life within the milk. A woman who buys pasteurized milk in the local market place is buying a very dubious quality, inasmuch as the milk is not very fresh as it arrives from the dairy; it has been kept in a low temperature that is quite likely to exceed far beyond the regulations of 25,000 bacteria organisms per cc. She may be buying very highly contaminated milk even though the label says pasteurized. Other products, such as ice cream are also found to contain a very high concentration of bacteria, some of which are of a very dangerous nature due to the element of human contamination.

A person who is coughing up sputum from his bronchi

or trachea is in no condition to handle foodstuffs of any kind; neither is a person who may go to remove the offal from the intestine without washing his hands before resuming his duties of handling food. There are many points of contamination along the lines of processing foods which may enter into, not only dairy products, but other products as well. "Food poisoning," in itself, is a very familiar quotation in your daily life. It is particularly prevalent in the somewhat careless handling of food, and the preparation of foods in these places. Even though city regulations are very stringent in these respects, yet, if the average individual were to compare the modern cafe with the antiseptic conditions of a laboratory or hospital, he would see the vast difference immediately. It is not possible to produce food and to properly prepare it for human consumption in large quantities in a cafe, where the elements of human contamination are so interjected from outside sources. Rats and cockroaches and numerous other types of contamination very often enter into the preparation of foods for humans.

The greatest source of contamination of foods for human consumption lies in the group of organisms which are commonly classified as bacillus. It is the clostridium bacillus which causes the so-called ptomaine poisoning which has been so properly associated with numerous other types of food poisoning. The true bacillus or ptomaine poisoning is 98 percent fatal when consumed in its true form. However, these bacillus organisms are the most prevalent germ life on the earth today. They are particularly abundant in the soil and in the fruits and vegetables which are eaten in a raw state upon the tables of the average American home. We can say that the average person eats large quantities of these very deadly germs, yet they do not at any time cause him any discomfort. It is simply because these germs have retired into a spore-like state and are not reproductive and therefore are not producing the toxemia which is the dreaded ptomaine poisoning.

Now, to further break down and enlarge your concept of germ life, you have all heard something of the enzymes and amino acids which are the building blocks in the construction of the protein elements in the human system. Your skin, your hair, and your fingernails are all protein substances and are extrusions of the alchemy of the body in reconstructing the protein amalgamated substances through the amino acids and enzymes which are used in the alchemy of the human system. Enzymes are classed as a by-product of this action of germs or bacteria upon certain protein substances which are contained in the food, or in such other foods as are in the intestinal system of the human body, and there is a very delicately balanced chemical transposition which to date has not been reproduced nor has it even been properly evaluated in the laboratory of your present day and time.

Your doctor of today does not really know what an enzyme is, nor does he know what a hormone is. He has a rough idea of what a vitamin is, although a vitamin is generally considered something of a catalyzing agent which enables certain processes of metabolism to enter into their normal function or relationship. Enzymes and their action with the amino acids in the system are equally important. I am not drawing the lines here between animal and man, and the processes in man's body are equally the same as in the smallest multi-celled animal that exists upon the earth today. We find very similar processes existing even into the smaller dimensions of the multi-celled creatures which exist as protozoans in the very low orders of function of the various species of the earth. Chemistry and alchemy are always entered into in direct action with either certain microscopic organisms or submicrobic organisms.

The scientist or doctor is concerned with virus; and yet there are virus within virus. We cannot convey to you the infinite nature of this concept. We know, very factually, that upon germs there are other germs which sometimes are capable of producing diseases in the germs, as the germs are capable of producing disease in the human body, and the element of size is just as great. Even with the advantages of the electronic microscope and magnifications of 20,000 or 30,000 diameters, the scientist could not even begin to approach the threshold of actually visualizing these super sub-microscopic germ worlds or dimensions which exist into the infinitudes of the sub-microscopic worlds.

Generally speaking, the scientist or the doctor of the earth could broaden the horizon of his concept into the metabolistic concept of the human body if he would begin to visualize the form and nature, the existence of energy and the transposition of energy into different dimensional forms which are immediately beyond the horizon of the physical inception. If the scientist could postulate such theories which would enable him to conceive that such structures as enzymes or hormones are somewhat in the nature of isotopes, but which he has somehow fathomed to be atomic structures, and the existence of isotopes and secondary derivations of atomic structures, existing in different dimensions of density in their relative atomic weights are indicative of such conditions which the scientist could arrive at should he pursue this same evaluation of concept in other fields of endeavor. In the field of biochemistry within the human body he would be able to factually relate these different dimensions of inceptions of energy in the transcendent understanding of how and why energy exists and in its transposition through different dimensions into such physical forms of relationship as are now immediately discerned by the physical senses. These concepts are factors which will relate man to his higher and more clairvoyant nature.

To associate clairvoyance with some state of trance, or witchcraft, or sorcery is something as fallacious and superstitious as tossing salt over your shoulder after tipping over the shaker on the table. Clairvoyance, as it exists to the scientist in the world of the future, will be a highly integrated science, which will relate him to the higher dimensions of his consciousness. He will, instead of stumbling upon a so-called discovery of certain elemental factors and relationships of nature, be able to actually tune himself into his superconscious state and in that state of consciousness, bring down into his physical world, the greater and super-abundance of knowledge which will expand the realm and dimension of his own finite world. And in the expansion and in the inception of such superconsciousness, he will be able to eliminate the great plagues and carriers of disease. He will be able to eliminate the hospitals and the asylums where people are placed more or less upon the rack of ignorance and torture, upon the wheel of reactionary existence. The world of reactionary expression will truly pass from the realm of man's conscious thinking and he will be able to integrate himself into such concepts as will make his world something which will be much closer to the oft' dreamed of, but never realized Utopia. This age is, as it has been mentioned in numerous transmissions, the New Aquarian Age or the building of the new City of Jerusalem. These factors are not spiritual concepts in their pure relative essence; they relate to a dimension and a time of expression on the earth when man will actually and factually be integrated with the higher concepts of life which are now so lacking.

Thus, it is our purpose here to span these dimensions in a rather unconventional manner and form. We are necessarily incurring the risk of antagonism which might well go along with trying to bring into the conscious domain of man's thinking the higher concepts of life, but as long as man is completely and thoroughly steeped in his dimension and in his time of physical science, he must be levitated out of such consciousness by, as we shall say, 'pulling on his own boot straps'. This he cannot do, and so we must do this for him. There must be brought into the consciousness of the scientist, the doctor, the philosopher, and the thinker, the newer and higher concepts of integration which will all automatically relate and interlock themselves into a harmonious conclusion of interpretations of concepts which will enable man to see the expression and nature of the Infinite God, as he so builds, rebuilds, manifests and expresses himself into the most minute and finite corner of the terrestrial dimension.

Until such future time, my dear ones, we will stand by ready to serve you.

— Louie.

CHAPTER XCII

Dear Friends — this is a most unusual opportunity and position for me, but first for identification; I am a former American, or rather I am still loyal to America, but, using the term 'former', as a citizen who lived in America and served America in rather an active way, both in the literary field and in the diplomatic service, I can be identified as the chap who left behind some of the American folk tales such as "The Legend of Sleepy Hollow" and the rather fantastic fable of "Rip Van Winkle" and his sleep. I also had the privilege of serving my country as an Ambassador to Spain, and, during that period of time, I became very interested in the religion known as Mohammedanism.

If you study the earth's history, you will see that most of the Mediterranean countries and even southern France and Germany were at one time occupied by the Turkish Empire, who are, of course, Moslems. It started somewhere about the twelfth or thirteenth century with a certain Turkish general by the name of Osman the First, who was guarding the borders of Turkey from Greece; and at that time the Byzantine Empire was still flourishing. There was, also, the Holy Roman Empire in France, Germany and other countries. Now this Osman started a campaign which ended in the next two or three hundred years with the various successors of the Turkish Caliphs and Emirs. As they were all very highly intelligent and strategically-minded gentlemen in the military field, they occupied most of the southern countries of Europe, which was known as the Ottoman Empire. They were, incidentally very tolerant of the Christian religion, which they called the religion of the infidels; as it was prohibited by the Moslem faith to forcibly convert people to their belief, the Christians were left pretty much alone, and I believe that is much more than would have been said had the circumstance been reversed.

During the many hundreds of years in the missionary fields, it seems like the Mohammedans and the Hindus have been trying to convert the Christians, and the Christians have been trying to convert the Moslems and the Hindus. A little later on I will give somewhat of a synopsis of this religion of Mohammedanism, and although there is a considerable amount of literature available at your time which deals with this very important religion, yet like the concept of Buddhism as well as the philosophy taught by Jesus, they have suffered considerable maligning and distortion down through the many centuries of time. When you arrive at some of these astral centers and study the histories of these different Avatars and descendants of the Holy men into the region of the terrestrial earth, you will see that they are somewhat perturbed at the derelictions of these very simple monotheistic doctrines. And so it is largely one of the purposes of this book to clear up some of the confusion in the existence of these various religions and to aid and to promote the freemasonry of the world. For, the understanding and relationship of the diverse religions and tearing down such deleterious concepts which have been interwoven or impinged into these different philosophies, man will be enabled to get to the core of the true philosophical religion which will actually relate him to his inner nature and will, of course, be a means of solving the greatest of his difficulties which is interracial relationship.

Before I get into this topic of conversation, I might say, incidentally, that I left a book behind on the earth which was called "Mohammed and His Successors", a book in which I gave a rather historical account of Mohammedanism as it existed on the earth at that time. However, the true facts as I am presenting them to you tonight, at this time, will be excerpts which could be said to have actually come from the lips of Mohammed, himself. He is one of the leaders of the Seventh Plane and, in that future time when you will be exploring that Center, he, himself, will enter somewhat more into the discussion of this religion as he brought it into existence on the earth at that time.

In this Center of Helianthus which is devoted to synthesis of inquiry and to education, I shall exercise the good old American prerogative of constructive criticism. Americans know a considerable amount of freedom in the expression of personal opinions which would not be tolerated under some of the other systems of government which have existed on the earth at different times. We, of course, would not fall under any jurisdiction from any governmental laws as they are exercised on the earth at this time, as we are quite beyond the reach of the effects of this jurisdiction.

However, we shall keep our constructive evaluations and criticism at a level which, we believe, will benefit the people who read these lines to such an extent that they will be able to formulate a definite policy and a basis of evaluation that will more constructively advance and progress their evolution. The civilization of America today is amazingly advanced in many of the technologies and techniques of the physical sciences — and we say it is amazingly so, because we are still just slightly puzzled as to how the American scientist has advanced to such a great point in his science — without including just a little more of the spiritual evaluation of the universe about him. He will, as a consequence, in the future, when he does finally unlock the door of the spiritual conceptions within himself, find that it will be something like opening the floodgate of the big Hoover Dam; or that he might, all of a sudden, knock the end out of a barrel and actually be flooded and precipitated with a veritable deluge of new knowledge and new technology which will automatically advance him very quickly and swiftly into a new prosperous era such as the earth has never known.

Looking about America today presents a very strange contrast to what it did in my time around the 1800's; and

I would be at a loss if I could choose which age to come back into, as this scientific age of yours is very fascinating. By the same token, all of the various and numerous advances in the technological sciences and in the evolution of home life should have, by consequence, advanced the level of existence of the American to a point which was now almost a veritable Utopia. However, it is always in the naturally ordained balances of mental levels in the evolution of man, that if he progresses more rapidly in one concept than in the mental faculties of the nation or civilization as a whole, it can not so keep up with the pace and there will be a condition of great unbalance created.

And in this unbalance will be found some very destructive forces which can and actually have precipitated a nation or a civilization into the abyss of gradual decline and oblivion. The mental level of the nations as a whole, and especially that of America, has not advanced to the point where they have been keeping up with the very rapid progress of the various technologies and sciences. There is, at the present time, a great and tremendous overbalance of this technology into the vast assassinations and the exploitations of the masses; and as it has been pointed out, this has given rise to numerous pressures which are sending hundreds of thousands of people to the asylums and to early graves, where, as in the ordinary sense of the word, they may have lived their lives in a perfectly tranquil state of existence, or into some such more orderly concept of life.

The mere idea of keeping up and continually compromising one's self with the thousands of numerous pressures, implications, advertising, exploitations, and such similar and kindred appearances of the present civilization is, in itself, one which could create a neurosis even by looking at it from where we are! So it is quite evident that it would take some sort of a supernatural mentality to completely compromise the various factors of your present civilization. A man must be either one of two things — he must be either this mental giant who can immediately compensate for all of these things, or he must run for the hills and find himself a very convenient cave, and isolate himself from all of these various pressures which he sees about him. Neither one of these solutions is practical, so we are trying to develop something of a synthesis for the average American whereby he can adopt a philosophical way of life which will insulate him, to some extent, from these various pressures.

You must know that America was conceived in its origin and in its beginning from the Centers of Shamballa as being one of the bulwarks against the vast seas of negative forces which are going to be, in a future day gradually rectified with the tremendous tides of new coming spiritual energy from higher and other dimensions of transition. That will all be part of creating the new 'so-called' Aquarian Age. The various processes of civilization in man's thinking, in the ordinary reactionary sense of the word, in itself, gives rise to the multitudes, in the hundreds of millions of people, and the sum and total of these negative expressions create these vast tides of astral energies which are swirling about the world at this time, and which must, in a future day, be rectified and returned to such a suitable form as will make it possible to re-use them in some future evolution of time. Energy, as you know, is a part of God, and is, in a general sense, in sum and total, indestructible. It is a transitional material and can be transferred from one dimension to another, or from a solid to a kinetic or dynamic form, or vice versa. But purely and simply, energy is not destroyed. In creating these tides of astral kinetic energy which swirl about the earth, man is, in his time, living in some sort of spiritual smog, which is much worse than that smog which is generated by the fumes of the exhaust pipes of the automobiles and which is being spewed from the factories and petroleum industries.

I would first like to get into some of the factors of the dietary system of the American public in particular. Some of these concepts, such as the harmful effects of the robot feeding of infants from the bottle, were entered into by a predecessor named Pasteur. The whole trend of the time is actually, in a sense of the word, to create people into actual machine-like robots. They are going about their numerous tasks in an every day sense, by the ticking motions of the clock; they must arise at a certain time, hurry down to the office or to the factory, turn out a specified amount of their various and numerous tasks and efforts and hurry home where they can rest so that they can get up and repeat the whole thing all over again. This, in itself, is something of a treadmill-like existence which is highly productive of neurosis. The acts of civilization, while they present, on the outside or the exterior surface, some very glittering attractions — the beautiful automobiles which swirl up and down the highways, the lighted windows of the numerous shops which display a vast and glittering assemblage of wares and artifacts of jewelry and household appliances — are, in themselves, creative of the very earnest desires in the breath and the mind of every passing individual.

The housewife, who does her shopping on the busy thoroughfare of an American city does so under the continual and abortive fact that she has a very limited budget. In looking at all of these vast and lovely arrays of merchandise, she must continuously shake her head, count the pennies in her purse and turn sadly away. This, in itself, will produce resentments which she must take out on her poor husband, or her children may also suffer something of the compromise which she is trying to arrive at or achieve in her mind. So, the husband must, in turn, take out his compromise on his fellow man in whatever field of endeavor in which he is related, and so this continual treadmill of emotional exchange goes on and on. One thing builds up to another. I would not have you believe in your minds that I am a misanthrope, that I dislike civilization, or that I dislike people; our opinions, as we express them here, are strictly from an objective viewpoint. We have arrived at the point where we do not become affected seriously, one way or another, with the evolutions and the various trials of mankind as he exists on the earth. While we are devoted and in the service to preserve his way of life, we do so in the full measure of a compassionate understanding; but it is one in which we can see much further ahead than the individual life of such of the many persons who go to make up the sum and total of such civilizations. We do not attach the importance to the small span of years of the mortal as he exists or lives on the earth, and as he is so wound up with himself in the expression of his few years; that, therefore, is only a small twinkling of his eye in the sum and total of the numerous evolutions of his existence. If he could be even partially far-sighted enough to see the unimportance of his existence on the earth, he might lose a lot of the urgent drives which force him into very unrelated factors of the expression of life in his terrestrial dimension. You know, it is a very interesting thing to view the American life as it exists today.

We could start out by saying we see the thousands and thousands of trucks which start out with their numerous and sundry cargoes in the very early and darkened hours of the morning; they start rolling towards the big cities, carrying their numerous loads of dairy products, poultry, meat, fish and other things which are necessary. The cities are like huge mouths and very hungry; they require tons and tons of foodstuffs to be poured down these hungry mouths every day. The way in which civilization of your time has contrived to feed these multitudes and masses of hungry mouths is, indeed, one of the amazing advances of your time.

In looking about in the different ways of the world, we can still see in India and China and in other Eastern and near Eastern countries, markets which are in existence and flourishing today just as they have been for thousands of years. There the various venders are carrying their numerous foodstuffs, just as their ancestors have carried on since the beginning of their civilization. Strolling through some of those market places, you would see woven baskets containing pigs, poultry, and numerous other types of livestock. You might also see huge heaps of different kinds of fruit and vegetables, and the owners of these piles of fruit standing patiently waiting for the nearest customer. Every morning the housewife or the servant of the palace must go to these markets and purchase the possible one or two meals in advance, and sometimes return for a second or third trip before the day is over. Usually, by the end of the day, and in the hot sun of the tropical countries, much of the foodstuff has suffered badly, as no one there knows what refrigeration is.

The average citizen of those Oriental or Eastern countries has developed a resistance to certain types of diseases which would very quickly kill the American, as the armies and navies, in going into these countries, found out during the last world war. The types of dysentery and venereal diseases which the average citizen of those countries has, and goes about hardly noticing, would kill an American in a few hours. Contrasting these market places, they indeed would cause the American housewife, doctor, scientist, or sanitation engineer to literally throw up his hands in holy horror.

We can picture the modern supermarket as it exists in the American city. Walking through the doors and going into this huge market, we will see the cleanliness, the sanitation and the utmost order and precision in the arrangement of the thousands of different types of foodstuffs on the shelves and bins. In walking up and down the aisles, looking at these various foodstuffs, we can say that, here, the problem of danger is actually reversed. If the Oriental or the Easterner could come into your supermarkets, perchance, and use many of the numerous foodstuffs which he saw upon the shelves, he might quickly begin to show signs of malnutrition. He would not be accustomed to the very highly refined and processed foods to which you have somehow built up some sort of resistance and immunity.

In looking at these numerous and brightly adorned packages and labeled articles in their sanitary cellophane and plastic bags, it is not possible to see that some of them are actually dangerous. It is a well-known and established fact among nutritionists and food experts of America, that about twenty-five percent of the people of your country are suffering from malnutrition. This is a strange paradox inasmuch as America is supposed to be the best fed nation of the world, and indeed this is so. The shelves, the granaries, and various places where food is produced, are literally bulging and overflowing. Also, the government pays farmers every year to plow their crops under or have them hauled out into the ocean and dumped because they cannot use the surplus of food!

Now, this, in itself, is another subject which I would like to discuss just a little more fully later on, but for the present, we shall investigate this supermarket which we have entered. Here is a section which is devoted to different types of flour. Now, most of the flour of your country is produced from wheat. Wheat in its natural state contains an outer layer which is called the bran, a second layer or cambium layer, which contains the most nutritional elements of the grain. In this cambium layer are found the vitamins and the minerals which are so necessary to sustain life. The interior of the wheat kernel is largely starch and gluten. Gluten is merely a form of protein. In refining this wonderful and beautiful white flour, the miller strips off both of these layers and also the little kernel of the wheat germ. The wheat germ has an oil which is literally nothing more than vitamin A. The remainder of the wheat, the gluten and starch is ground up and bleached, and usually formed into some sort of a chlorine or a lime by-product, which is, in essence, highly poisonous. Chickens will starve to death in three days time on a diet of white flour. The miller has felt a little guilty in depriving his fellow citizen of all of the nutritional elements of the wheat, so he slyly sneaks in a little bottle of vitamin B and another little pill of iron and puts on the label of the bag of flour that it is 'enriched'. The baker who uses this flour to make the numerous loaves of bread wrapped in bright packages will also print on them 'enriched'.

Now, this word 'enriched' is very misleading as the small amount of iron, or vitamin A and B which is added, does not in any way compensate for the vitamins and minerals which have been stripped from the grain.

Here, next to the flour is the sugar bin; sacks and bags and packages of sugar — most all of it with hardly an exception — is white sugar. That means that in the process of manufacturing, a certain percentage of lime has been interjected into the sugar crystals to bleach the brown or molasses part, which remained after a certain process was completed. This refined or purified white sugar is almost indigestible in the human system.

Passing on into another section, you see brightly labeled metal containers, which are called tin cans, containing the different fruits; here again, has been entered into, some more of that processing. Most all of these fruits have been peeled which means that the outer skin layers which are, in themselves, laxative in nature, have been stripped off from the fruit, along with a good portion of the vitamins and minerals, which are also contained in the cambium layer on the outside of each peach or apricot or whatever the fruit may be. The metal container is, in fact, something which is very destructive to vitamin C. The mere contact of a grapefruit knife in paring and cutting the sections of grapefruit for your morning breakfast, will destroy about 75 percent of the vitamin C of that grapefruit. The vegetables, too, have suffered some processing and some contamination. We must not forget for one moment that many of these fruits and vegetables have been grown in orchards or in soil which has been in very concentrated production for many years. Usually, nothing has been added to the soil other than a few phosphates. Actually, most of the minerals and vitamins have long ago been bleached from the soil through the process of growing numerous crops, so that these fruits and vegetables have arrived at the canning plants as nothing more than effigies of what a fruit really should be.

Here are some packages of rice. Now, rice is a staple food of many of the Asiatic and Eastern countries. In its natural state, rice is very much like the wheat, containing a rough outer bran layer and an inner cambium layer which is full of minerals and vitamins. In stripping off and polishing this rice, it has suffered just the same as the wheat. The corn meal which you see on the shelf has also suffered somewhat the same drastic fate. The elimination of the small germ cell, along with the oil and the vitamin which it contained, has likely converted corn meal to nothing more or less than a starchy substance. Even the bran which is so necessary and vital for some sort of roughage in the intestinal tract, too, has been lost. Formerly these products, or the extractions from the grains were fed the livestock, and, as a consequence, the livestock were very well fed. Now, however, these different refining processes are used in chemistry to manufacture and extract the vitamins and minerals

1029

which are again sold back to the public in fancy bottles at very fancy prices as vitamin supplements.

Another word about vitamin supplements would be in order; a chemist can synthesize certain vitamins, especially the B complex type. Although, in most cases, the natural vitamins are quite naturally the best to use, it cannot be said that any manufactured vitamin or synthesized vitamin is, in any sense of the word, equal to the original product. There are different reasons for this; the most important one is, that through the processing of these chemicals which enter into the manufacture of the vitamin, various metals are contacted and, in themselves, destructive to certain psychic qualities of the vitamin.

This word 'psychic' quality is a concept which I would like to enter into, as it is very important in remembering what you actually take into your bodies, in the way of food. We could begin by saying you take a drink of water from the faucet; now, this water has run through miles of metal pipes. The iron, itself, is a metal which can very easily be magnetized. Magnetic structures exist in many different forms and dimensions, just as in other relationships of energies. Some of these magnetic structures are psychic in nature and exist in relationship to certain psychic qualities of the individual's makeup. In other words, the psychic energies of the water which runs through the pipe have in coming in contact with the metal, been largely dissipated or discharged. The water is not as useful a substance in the body as it formerly could have been, had it been supplied directly from a spring from the ground or from some stream high in the mountains.

You could further simplify this concept by assuming that all foods — whether water or in any other form which you eat or take into your body — are atomic structures and consequently energy which has to be converted.

As in the case of isotopes, the energies in the atomic structures are not only contained in the atoms which compose the numerous molecules of the different foods which you eat, but you are also consuming a large quantity of such substances which we might call isotopes — in other words, they are psychic atoms which exist in the higher orders of frequency relationships, just as atoms do exist in the different elements and are related to their own atomic structures. To make a long and rather technical discussion simple and short, it would be best to remember that the more natural the source of food, in relationship to the individual, is by consequence, the most vital and related process and one from which the individual derives a much greater amount of nourishment.

Sustaining the human body is merely a process of reinstating enough energy back into a usable or transferable form. When you have progressed into the astral dimensions, you will know that such usable energy as you need in your daily life will not be assimilated from the alimentary canal; as you will then have none. Neither will you need the oxygen you breathe which is used as an aid in the metabolism of the body, as you will have no lungs. The mere act of eating and breathing to sustain life in your dimension is one which links you with the lower orders of animal and the earth plane existence. As a direct consequence, the process of eating and breathing should be simply followed through in its closest relationship. The further one deviates from this path of relationship, as far as the body is concerned, the more the body will suffer from different types of malnutrition.

There are many kinds of malnutrition which are not measured in the general sense or term of the word or can be detected by the physical, such as the more extreme cases of malnutrition, as they are expressed in physical forms of beri-beri, as it was known by the mariners, or to various other types of bodily decomposition, which set in simply from lack of certain vitamins and minerals. In reinstating these vitamins as substances back into the body, the individual rapidly recovers. However, these related the individual to the metabolism of the body in a purely physical form. There are other types of malnutrition which are somewhat in a more related or psychic form. The psychic centers and the psychic body itself can suffer very seriously if certain psychic elements and atomic structures are not eaten by the individual. Strange to say, but not all of the energy which you derive and use in your psychic body is from the astral or higher dimensions. Much of the energy which is used in the lower orders of subconscious reflexes are contained in these organic substances — called food. You will be able to prove this to yourself much more easily as you will see that many of the psychosomatic disturbances which children have been experiencing in eating various foods, actually developed into very strong neuroses in later years, simply because the foods which they were forced to eat did not contain certain psychic elements.

The children being a little wiser than the parents in the matter of being closer to, shall I say, an instinctive or psychic relationship with their true selves, rebelled or revolted against the idea of eating certain foods for the simple reason that the child instinctively knew that this food did not contain the right psychic elements. A little thought on this concept will easily convince you that eating foods is something more than making an effort to balance your budget from the commissary of the supermarket. A housewife must be very conscientious in selecting the various foodstuffs in the large varieties which are at her disposal; and that in selecting these foods, she must always bear in mind that she is trying to evaluate a certain balance in the calories, such as are termed the carbohydrates, the proteins, fats, the starches, etc. However, she must always, in the selection of these foods in the supermarket, by consequence, select either partially or fully processed foods. Do not think for one moment that because there are frozen foods in the large bins of a refrigerator that these foods are any better either, or are of a higher food value than any of the other foods which are so processed. The act of freezing is just as serious in destroying vitamins and altering other foodstuffs as is boiling. The extremes of temperature in either case are exceedingly destructive. Furthermore, rapid thawing and returning the food to a high temperature of boiling, creates another extreme which also alters the vitamin and mineral constituents and bleaches them out into the water which is usually drained down the sewer.

It has been said that in America, the drain pipe is the best fed mouth in the world, and this is literally true. If the American housewife spent much less time slaving over the kitchen stove to prepare the numerous dishes by such cooking and processing, her family would be much better off and they would be much more properly fed than from the different developments of the highly processed dishes which she manages to contrive. Another very fallacious thing which some housewives do — and they are not particularly housewives, but other business women — they must return hurriedly from their various jobs or positions; they go to the pantry and grab a few pans and do a little opening with the can opener with the result that some such concoctions are placed upon the table which give rise to a great deal of dyspepsia and to a large amount of irritation with the other members of the family who are forced to eat these very hurriedly and often unrelated and unbalanced meals.

The future problem of dietetics of the nation must be a problem which will have to be solved in a somewhat more realistic fashion than by continually processing foods and re-emphasizing new short cuts to preparing meals quicker, so that the American mouth can be fed with food which is more nutritional and contains not only the basic elements of the various vitamins and minerals but which also contains the numerous psychic elements of which the earth scientist is not yet quite aware. These concepts are just beyond his immediate horizon in the future evolution of the earth, and in his science as it exists, just as he has found in the hormones and enzymes, as they are manufactured and used, or as they are manifest in the human body, they are very necessary and mysterious agents which are somewhat catalytic in nature. In recent years the scientist and chemist developed an artificial cortisone, or as it is termed 'ACTH', which is used so widely in treating arthritis.

Arthritis is a disease of frustration and disappointment; any person who has suffered a large dose of sudden bereavement or disappointment in life, is subject to arthritis in some later period of his life. The various incurable indispositions of the human body present to the doctor problems which have been, up until now, unsolved simply because he has not penetrated beyond the borderline of the physical body. He has visualized the origin of these conditions as being in the physical body and has, therefore, not arrived at their true cause which is strictly psychic in nature, and which usually develops through a combination of bad nutrition, not only from the physical standpoint but from the mental standpoint as well.

If a person's philosophy of life is not sufficiently substantial to enable him to go through a period of time which separated him from a loved one in what is called death in a more normal way, he can manufacture a condition in the physical body known as arthritis. It is well known that a person who worries and nags very frequently develops stomach ulcers, and it is generally conceived by the earth doctors and scientists that most all of the human ailments can somehow be traced to the emotional values of life as they are manifest in your civilization at this time. So, as direct consequence, the pure and curative values do not come from the test tube or the scalpel, but they must come from a civilization which begins to live closer to the true functional orders of dispensation as they have been so conceived in the Immortal Mind of the Creator. Deviations from the pure channel of relationship from the Infinite Self always lead to disastrous results if these deviations are continued for any length of time. This is true, not only in the dietary sense, but is very true in a psychic or a mental sense. Deviates are not only sexual or mental, but they can also be dietary as well as in many other types of human relationships. As a consequence of these numerous deviations, the masses of humanity, as a rule, soon develop certain predominances of character which are always characteristic of the time and age in which the person or race of man so lived and existed at that time.

The numerous artifacts of civilization are literally producing a type of man which — while it is indigenous to its particular evolution — will be one which can be very definitely marked by future archeologists, who may dig beneath the surface of the earth and uncover, at some future time, some remnants of this present civilization; he will look at the skeletons and at the traces of this civilization and he will mutter under his breath and sadly shake his head and say such things as "Well, the poor people," and, "How badly they had strayed in their efforts for civilization." You may well imagine that people on other planets who have advanced somewhat in a position of social structures which are very superior to your own, at your present day, may be looking down their noses on their long-ranged telescopes, and they, too, are sadly shaking their heads and muttering under their breath, and hoping in some way that they can shake you all loose for just a few minutes time from what looks like a very mad race to oblivion; and well it may become such a mad race.

The numerous artifacts of civilization were primarily contrived as instruments for convenience. These various inventions are immediately seized upon by the diverse manufacturing concerns so that they may be manufactured and turned out in vast numbers at competitive prices, and, as a consequence, the American public suffers a great deal of exploitation. These numerous contrivances and artifacts have, as I have said, created a strange paradox. While they should have contributed considerably towards the easement and relief of some of the more laborious aspects of life, they have, however, actually reverted man back to a process to sustain this civilization so that he must exert much more mental and physical effort than he would normally be required to do if he had followed a simpler path of life. You may think for a moment that the farmer who, fifty or a hundred years ago, arose at the crack of dawn with the crowing of the cock, tilled the fields behind the plow with the old grey mare, milked the cow, and tended the chickens, was leading a very laborious life; but this was not so. He was very happy in his way of life; he raised a large family and they usually all lived to be a ripe and happy old age; they spent many hours around the fireside, celebrating the Christmas festivals, the Thanksgiving time and numerous holidays of the American tradition.

Christmas time in America is a time which has become somewhat of a nightmare to most American housewives, and to the fathers as well. To rush madly about from shop to shop, what to get for Harry, or what shall I buy for Jane, or all of a sudden a half dozen new presents or possibilities or reciprocations have appeared on the horizon stems from the old idea of keeping up with the Joneses. Christmas, as it exists in America today, is not the traditional Christmas that existed a hundred years ago. By the time Christmas day arrives most members of the household are too exhausted to enjoy Christmas as it should be enjoyed. Christmas time should be a time of observance of spiritual contemplation just as Thanksgiving was contrived and devised too, as a period of thanksgiving to our Creator and supplier of all man's needs. Christmas should be a time which is remembered and meditated upon in the elements of Christianity, as they have been so contained and interwoven into the American way of life. It should not be the hustle, worry, and bustle, or the idea of reciprocation as to who can buy the best gifts to exceeding one's budget, or to incurring debts and committing oneself to numerous financial obligations which will further worry and encumber him. These ideas and practices are nonsensical and entirely without foundation, for the true Christmas should be as it formerly existed in America during the time of the Puritans, or up until the beginning of the age of machinery.

In my time, the Christmas custom was one to which we all looked forward, not with dread or a vague sense of some sort of impending doom, or overwork or catastrophy; but rather, we looked forward to Christmas with something of a reverence and respect in our hearts for perpetuating in the minds and the American way of life, the idea of inception of the Mission of Jesus into the world and to what His Mission really meant to the races of people who have since come to know His philosophies.

The subject of Christianity, itself, is one which would bear a great deal of discussion, and one in which I would like to participate. However, I will leave that up to the powers that regulate these great Centers, and I believe that I have given as much here as can possibly be utilized at this particular moment. So, until such further continuance — God Bless you all there in America.

— Washington Irving.

P.S. — Good day again folks; I believe we were walking through a large supermarket and discussing some of the relative values of the many goodies which we saw about us, and the diet of the average American citizen; we have found that, just as in many ways of life, considerable amounts of synthetics and processing have been entered into, which were rather deleterious to the proper assimilation and nutritional elements which should have been contained in the food. As Pasteur pointed out, pasteurizing milk partially destroyed some of the food values and the elements necessary for the full realization of the food value of milk; so, the numerous products of the farm and country which you see here in the markets are also, to a large extent, very highly processed and refined. The sugars which are used in some of these foods have a two-fold effect inasmuch as they are very acid producing, and can, with the mixture of saliva, be positively caustic upon tooth enamel. This is especially true with the sugars used in the soft drink industry; and there is a common complaint among teenagers, using a word which I will not mention for obvious reasons, that they have a soft drink tooth decay age. Also, as we studied the processing of the fruits and vegetables, it was evident that much of the roughage had been eliminated by this processing, and, as a consequence, teeth and gums suffered from lack of polishing and stimulation.

Going along a little further in this market we see a very large display counter which is devoted to the various meat products. The subject of meat, in itself, is rather a touchy one, and is liable to produce great controversy. We may say that man is omnivorous or that he has a very highly adaptable intestinal tract which is capable of digesting all types of foodstuffs whether vegetable, fruit, or the meat variety. Contrasting, as we have said, the picture of the Eskimo who lives almost entirely upon a meat or fat diet, with that of the various sects in India, which prohibit even the consumption of fertilized eggs, we see, in these countries to eat meat, would be a very horrifying and vilifying act.

Going into Japan, we see here too that, like the coastal areas of China, most of the meat is of the fish variety which comes from the sea, and very little if any livestock of any kind is used or is consumed. In the more interior regions of China, a considerable amount of pork is eaten among the sects of those who are not Buddhists. It must be borne in mind that in these countries the temperatures are rather hot and are, in themselves, prohibitive factors in the production and consumption of meat, as there is little or no refrigeration generally in use in marketing these various foodstuffs in a public or open market.

As for yourself, you may choose whether or not you like to consume a certain amount of meat, as it is a very valuable supply of proteins and generally speaking, the various laws and regulations from the government make it reasonably certain that most meats are in a good and satisfactory condition for consumption. Choose your meats wisely, however, and remember that in the case of rather sickened animals, very large concentrations of staphylococcus organisms can exist. There are seven or eight varieties of these organisms that can make a person very ill and even cause death. There is also a universally known and prevalent condition, especially among the swine, called trichina, which is a very small worm-like animal inhabiting the flesh of hogs. However, beef is not entirely immune from trichina; it is also sometimes found in poultry, turkeys, and even in fish. So, here again, a very wise selection and a thorough cooking is in order. It must be remembered that trichina can be killed by raising the temperature of the meat to about 180 degrees fahrenheit for a duration of three minutes time.

Now we are up in front of this supermarket into the section which is devoted to fruits and vegetables. We will point to some of the rather fallacious interpretations in which the average housewife can indulge herself. She believes that if she serves a cooked vegetable and a salad along with the main dish, which is usually meat, she is reasonably sure her family is properly nourished. Let us examine some of the fruits and vegetables which are at this counter. We will begin with these two carrots first, and we will call one 'A' and the other 'B'. 'A' carrot comes from the soil which is almost virgin and is very rich in humus qualities, while carrot 'B' has come from soil which has grown many crops of carrots as well as other vegetables so that this soil is almost depleted in vitamin and mineral elements. As you can see in breaking down the chemical analysis, the difference between 'A' carrot and 'B' carrot would reveal that the latter carrot had little or no vitamin and mineral content while carrot 'A' could be fairly crammed with these nutritional elements. It must also be borne in mind that after pulling the carrot from the ground, even an hour's exposure to sunlight and air will oxidize a large quantity of the vitamin A as well as some of the vitamin C.

Looking about to the different types of vegetables such as the cabbages, lettuce, asparagus and other leafy crops which are grown above the ground, these too, could be grown in soil which is relatively deficient in minerals and vitamins. However, there are other dangers to these crops which are grown above the ground which must also be remembered. During the last few years, your political system has been combating or fighting a 'cold war' with a foreign nation, while the entomologist or the scientist in America and in other civilized countries has also been fighting a 'cold war' against the insect world. If it were not for the great amount of research work done by these combating agencies through the agricultural department of the U.S, it is quite possible that America could have starved to death before now. And it is entirely conceivable that in the future, unless new insecticides and new methods are found to combat many of these numerous pests, the possibility of starving to death is not entirely remote. The new aggregation of sprays and insecticides are designed to kill, not only our local pests which have lived on this continent for hundreds of years, but also numerous other pests and such imports as the Japanese Beetle or the Gypsy Moth which flourished in Europe. Ladybugs are being grown to destroy the aphis and other types of plant life upon which the Lady Beetle feeds. The scientists have also developed some very powerful sprays, something on the lindane or chloride natures which are not only very poisonous to insects, whether they touch them or whether they eat them, but they are also very poisonous to humans.

It is usually safe to say that most vegetables and fruits reach the market in a somewhat contaminated condition from these numerous sprays, and it is not only unsafe but absolutely necessary as a precautionary measure, to thoroughly wash and soak off any residual sprays as may be clinging to the fruits or the leaves of these vegetables. At the present time, statistics would show you that while it has been suppressed, yet, nevertheless it is a fact that large masses of the city population are suffering from the effects of some sort of partial poisoning from some of these very highly poisonous sprays. The old arsenic of lead has not entirely been displaced and, that too, as you know, is a very poisonous product. So do be careful and thoroughly wash all your fruits and vegetables before eating.

The subject here too, of fruits and vegetables is something which can be further discussed. There is a common practice of picking some of the fruits and vegetables before they have reached maturity, that is, before they are fully ripened. They are picked at the height of their size, and in some cases are artificially colored to produce the necessary glow or attractive quality which is necessary for their sale. The fact that fruits and vegetables are sometimes picked this way is a method of insuring that through the lengthy process of shipping and marketing these products, they shall not suffer from spoilage and rotting. It is obvious that an apple, a peach, or a pear, if it is picked before fully ripened, will market in a much better condition than would a fully ripened fruit. However, the partially ripened fruit or vegetable is not, in any sense, the same kind of fruit which is ripened upon the tree, as anyone who has visited an orchard or a farm where these products are grown and has eaten the tree or vine-ripened fruit will know by comparison that there is considerable difference. Tomatoes, for instance, are picked even before they are of a reddish color, and a certain gas is placed in the refrigerator cars which will color these tomatoes a very beautiful red. They are, however, inferior to the vine-ripened tomatoes, both in food value, in taste, and also in quality. Vine-ripened tomatoes must be marketed within a few hours or they are liable to suffer considerable damage from softening and spoilage. This is quite true with peaches and pears. Apples, however, do not suffer quite so much as most varieties grown, are naturally of a rather hard or a firm texture and are usually picked at almost their peak of perfection.

There is, as I have said, considerable difference between the tree-ripened fruit and that which is sometimes found in the markets, so that by eating some of the fresh fruits you find in the market does not insure you of your full quota of vitamins and minerals, as very often these vitamins and minerals do not make their full appearance until the last few days of the ripening process due to the energies or actinic rays of the sun with the last act of nature in the tree itself, in placing these vitamins and minerals within the outer layers of the fruits. I have really no suggestion at the present time which would eliminate these evils that are primarily produced and instigated with the desire of producing foods from the country which are attractive to the eye of the housewife who purchases these items for her family. She does so mainly on the basis that they appear very attractive, but as she has no way of making a chemical analysis, she does not, therefore, know that these things are not as they are represented. She is, if I can use the good old American slang expression, 'buying a pig in a poke'. She must choose these foods in a more or less haphazard fashion.

The stalk of bananas which you see hanging there is quite useless for food in a comparative fashion to the natural tree-ripened banana which you might find in the tropical countries where the natives pick them from the tree just as mother nature ripens them in the full tropical sun. Those bananas were picked when they were quite green, and, in the shipping and storing, the fruit could only extract or convert certain types of sugars, the elements of which were actually contained in the small stalk to which they had grown. Therefore, the bananas are of an entirely different texture and taste from those which you would find growing in the same region and which were ripened in the tropical sun.

Usually, in most cases, public opinion is a tremendous and a mighty weapon, yet, the housewife becomes cognizant of the fact that she is paying very good money for something which she does not actually receive. She may be so incited as to raise some sort of a hue and cry, wherein legislation could be enacted so that the fruits and vegetables, as well as other products which are consumed on the table, would have to be packaged and marked with the reasonable assurance that they contained certain vitamins and certain minerals; then the housewife could buy these products from the standpoint and on the basis that this bunch of carrots in a cellophane bag was reasonably protected from oxidation and that it was grown in soil which made it possible to analyze the carrot for a certain percentage of vitamin A or carotene. The same labels and packaging would, of course, be quite effective in all types of fruits and vegetables whether they were canned or purchased in a fresh state.

The packaging and labeling of meats and other types of foods, too, could follow in a rather short and rapid order if the housewife and the purchaser became sufficiently aware of the various and glaring defects in the producing and marketing of the foodstuffs which are eaten upon the table. This legislation and a consequential amount of enacting, and the expense entailed in labeling and producing these packages of food would quite necessarily raise the prices somewhat; however, I do believe that this would be entirely justifiable, inasmuch as the health of the nation, as a whole, would be quickly improved. It is commonly judged among medical circles and life insurance companies that America is, as a whole, the healthiest nation in the world. These statistics very often, are quite likely to be misleading and have been taken or based upon some comparatively recent level where sanitation and various other factors were not relevant in making such statistics available.

There are many races of people living on the earth today who have not had the sanitation or the awareness of the scientific marvels of vitamins and minerals, but they are magnificent specimens of humanity. There are natives living in Africa who have never bathed in their lives; they rub their bodies with a mixture of various fats or oils; and, as any explorer can tell you, if the wind is right, you can tell that they are around as far as a half mile away; yet, these natives very often reach a ripe old age without losing a single tooth and are very rugged, strong individuals even in their nineties and in their hundreds! They usually subsist upon whatever nature is convenient in delivering by way of the spear or the trap or they may even in time of necessity, consume large quantities of caterpillars or insects which abound about the face of the country.

There is one tribe of natives living upon a certain lake in Africa who make cakes of gnats which abound and literally clog the air so that it is impossible to see, to any degree, more than a few feet away; they make these small cakes of gnats and actually consume them. It was the custom of many Indians to make a meal of dried grasshoppers which was considered very delicious; it was made into cakes or into porridge and tasted something like shrimp. I am merely mentioning these things to point out some contrast as to how the average American citizen in your present time and age, prides himself, and justifiably so, on the tremendous resources and the facilities of sanitation, and feeding the mouths of these large cities of America. This is practically the only way in which it could be done. To transport and market food in such large quantities in any other way, except in a rather extremely sanitary way, would be almost prohibitive; however, the elements of processing foods and making them sanitary are, to be sure, quite often very destructive to the numerous vitamins and minerals which nature has usually impounded within these food products. The remedy here, as I have suggested, means that both elements of sanitation and processing, as well as to be fully aware of the innermost nutritional values of food, must be combined with their growing and also the distribution. The American consumer should be made thoroughly aware that he is buying such merchandise, that he is entitled to what he pays for, and that it is useless to eat food unless it does contain the proper nutritional elements.

You would not wear clothing which did not fully protect you or would not meet with the standards of society in the time and place in which you are at present residing; nor, would the average American live in a hut which was fashioned from straw and sticks as do many of the savages and the primitive peoples in the jungles. These things are products of a very highly civilized and a very mechanized world. The borders of such civilization, however, can be pushed to such an extent that they may actually, in a sense, kill off the very race of people who had so instigated and brought about their fullest extent and realization. (The railroad train was passing nearby at this point.) My, you do live in a noisy world, don't you. Great difficulty is sometimes experienced in talking above the roar of those iron monsters which go past the house. I understand that they, too, produce large quantities of different types of chemical elements in the air which are called smog and are very injurious to the respiratory tract of the average human. This, too, is a problem which will have to be solved in order that large masses of people will not actually be converted into very sick or otherwise incapacitated people. However, I do believe that I have covered the subject of foods and marketing in your cities to some extent. Please bear in mind that I have presented these factors to you so that you can more suitably prepare the various meals of the day to feed the mouths of the loved ones around you, and that you may be better able to nourish yourself.

I have not gone into this subject to point out or to criticize but rather to try to help you prevent what could be very serious and highly repercussive effects in the consumption of the highly processed foods which, in many cases, contain little or no food value in themselves. There are many other elements which enter into the life of the average city dweller, for foods of any kind must be consumed only at times when a person is comparatively relaxed and without nervous tension, so that the blood may fully circulate around the digestive tract, and peristalsis can proceed in a fully energetic manner and pattern. The girl who rushes from the office into the nearby drugstore and consumes some fancy sundae or two slices of very lightly charred white bread, which she calls toast, wherein is placed a little mixture of mayonnaise and tuna, is not doing her body very much good. She is filling her stomach, to a certain degree, with something which will cause the stomach to cease its contractions or hunger pangs, but she will likely begin to suffer from numerous types of malnutrition; and along with the habit of smoking a pack or two of cigarettes, this girl can very quickly be led to the nearest hospital.

I would thoroughly advocate that the working day of the individual begin with a morning shift of about three hours duration and a two-hour intermission at noontime wherein a light lunch of such fresh fruits and vegetables could be suitably eaten, followed by a period of complete relaxation for possibly an hour, with a resuming of the duties for another three or four hours. The hurrying and scurrying, and hustle and bustle of the modern civilized way of life is one which is breaking down the health of many millions of people, and filling the hospitals and asylums with all kinds and types of physically and mentally ill people who have arrived in such a state simply because of the wrong eating and thinking habits. As a former American, I am still very much interested in the welfare of my country and would in a future day, like to see many of the elements which are in full sway at the present time, be displaced by more healthy attitudes and ways of life which would develop the mental and physical health of the country to a comparative degree, which was in keeping with the general trend of the times. However, I must not stay too long at this time.

For the immediate future we will shortly close this section of Shamballa, and you will again be conducted to the opening of a new section; but before this is done, there will be some other sort of a suitable exploration and resume of the final and concluding chapters of this section. May I say in closing that I have been most happy to again come into the presence of some of my fellow countrymen in whatever capacity that I could best serve them, and until such future day when I can again make some sort of an appearance or comment, if this could be possible, I remain yours.

— Washington Irving.

CHAPTER XCIII

This is Eliason; I am most happy to welcome you back to Helianthus. If you recall, I assisted in one or more transmissions in the beginning of this book; and if you so remember, my place is natively here in the number two section of Helianthus; serving in conjunction with the executive departments in the main section of Parhelion, which is devoted largely to the synthesis and the educational systems, and in derivatives of different types of analysis which would serve mankind best in his own respective dimension. I am most particularly interested in the children and those youngsters who have passed from the earth in, shall I say, a rather incomplete cycle of reincarnation. They are sometimes brought to this center of Helianthus where they are assisted in gaining their educational background and other facilities of that nature which will enable them to further progress or to reincarnate into some suitable earth plane dimension.

Now that you find yourself sitting in the large park-like area which is immediately in front of the great Temple, we will sit quietly here upon the bench beside this pool while you can become better accustomed to the beauty and brilliance which is about you. Just as in previous explorations, the beautiful vistas of the radiant pulsating Heavens above you are glowing; there is the feeling of warmth and abundance, of security and peace of mind and complacency in all things. We here have been quite busy, may I say, in the last few days — if I can use the term 'days' — for we know nothing of the value of time as in your earth dimension; but with the quickening of the Christmas spirit in the terrestrial earth, there is a considerable amount of extra activity which comes into these various Centers of Unarius, as they are associated in a more personal relationship with numerous individuals who have passed into some position in that planetary aspect. However, it must be borne in mind that we, too, are concerned with several other thousand planets, and that they, too, have their own cycles of spiritual manifestation wherein there are other festive occasions of a somewhat spiritual nature so that by and large, with a moments thought, you will see that we do not have much time here for becoming idle; we are constantly in contact with any number of planets which are engaging at the moment in some form of religious observance.

To the earth dweller, the period of Christmas is one which is more strictly an astrophysical concept, and relates as it does to the passing of the earth through a certain meridian which is known as the winter solstice. This winter solstice is on the 21st day of December;in the concept of pure science, it can be said that the earth passes through a large line of magnetic force on that particular day, so that with the conjunction of this magnetic force with the earth, we are enabled at that time, during the brief period of several earth days to project into the earth much energy of the Radiant nature, which is sometimes called spiritual, which means so much and is of such great value to the dweller in the lower terrestrial dimensions.

It must be borne in mind, however, that the observance of the Christmas season, as the birth of Jesus, is one which is somewhat subject to discussion and debate. The original concept of Christianity and its inception into the world at the time of Paul was one into which was interwoven many cults or religious systems as they existed on the earth at that time. The reason for this being that there must be, by necessity, a large amount of mysticism or esoterical value in such religions which would appeal to the people; as mankind, in general, is rather superstitious by nature, and has, in his more elemental state of living, been somewhat reactionary to the mysterious forces of nature.

The exact birthdate of Jesus at the particular time of December the 25th, is merely a parable in itself, and should not be taken as the exact calendrical date which is given in the Gregorian concepts of your time. It refers rather to an advent of the dying of the old year and the beginning of the new year. Such observances of this nature have been in existence among the races of mankind since the beginning of concepts wherein man was enabled to visualize the passing of different seasons and various times so that he had thus instituted in his way of life somewhat of an astrological or astrophysical concept wherein he regulated his days or seasons according to such concepts as existed within his mind, as he witnessed the transmissions of nature about him. Usually, a study of the histories of the earth will acquaint you with the facts that many people who are in existence on the earth today still have similar observances of the period of the winter solstice; just as are in existence concepts which also embody the Easter period, which is sometimes known as the Spring Festival or the Spring Equinox. There is, likewise, the Fall Equinox in September which is also observed by many races of people upon the earth.

I would, also at this time, remind the people that they have somewhat neglected, and rather sadly, the true nature and the true value of the Christmas observance. It has degenerated into a complete debacle of rushing, hurrying and scurrying around in buying and wrapping packages, and in relying too much on whether or not someone is remembering the person and that reciprocation must be entered into. "If someone does not buy me a gift, why should I buy him one?" The idea of gift giving in itself, is one which had its origin in giving the incense and myrrh to the infant Jesus in the story of the New Testament. However, it would be a much greater and better thing if people could give spiritual gifts of love and kindness and observance to each other and to remember each other, not only at the Christmas season, but all the remaining days of the year in a likewise manner and fashion. The Christmas observance, as exists, would be one which could be a reminder for the general populace of mankind to continually reciprocate this Christmas spirit of love and kindness among themselves in their future lives together on their planet.

So that, by and large, and especially in America, Christmas is, of today, commercial or reactionary in nature, and has lost much of its true esoterical value in promulgating or promoting the true spiritual contact within the nature of the individual who believes in the Christian pageantry. I would like to point out, also, that the worship of Jesus is contrary to that which He, Himself set about to teach when He was on the earth. His entire philosophy teaches — not one in which He should be worshipped — but rather, He reminded people to love one another as they loved themselves, and that each should love his God with all his heart and soul. In misinterpreting or implying any sense of personal worship to the man Jesus would be quite contrary to His wishes and one which would also be quite contrary to a true Christian concept. Rather, we should recognize the Christ Consciousness which is within each individual, and that his Christ Consciousness is the true God Self of the individual. This was so strongly pointed out and emphasized by Jesus, that each individual possesses this same embodiment, the same qualities, the same virtues of the God Self, just as He Himself possessed them. It was in living with, and in closer continuity with this contact, that He was able to bring into the world a very high spiritual philosophy. I believe, however, this subject has been rather adequately covered in several other places and in different transmissions.

In general, to this plane of synthesis and inquiry and into the educational values and nature of the world about you, there have been many subjects which we have touched upon, which we believe, by this objectivism, that you can best orient yourself into a more compatible state of life. The numerous pressures of law, order and social structures, as they exist about you in your reactionary world, as it has been so strongly emphasized, have given rise to tremendous pressures which are felt by every individual. We have not yet touched upon some of the other aspects of the life and the world about you, which I will try to do rather briefly before we begin the exploration of the temple, itself, at this time. I wish to take you into the temple and show you the interior, as it is very important that you should know the nature of the observance of Christmas as it is portrayed from these various Centers.

We have discussed, in part, the penal systems and institutions in the world about you, and emphasized rather strongly that the present corrective measures are only ways of trying to correct some very obvious fault which lies within the individual; that it has not occurred after he has become an adult but rather these corrective measures should be entered into while one is still a child! The ounce of prevention here is likewise recommended.

Speaking of the educational systems as children are taught in the schools about you, there has been some advancement in the buildings and in the extent to which the educational systems have been instituted in your civilization; yet they are but a step removed from the medieval times of the dark ages during the period of the Reformation. Just as are the penal institutions, and just as are the systems of psychiatry and medicine but a step in advance of these systems which were in use but a short period of time before. There is still much room for improvement in the educational systems as they exist for the children and the growing youngsters and teenagers of your time and day. I would remind you that the idea of vocational guidance is one which obviously has been rather sadly neglected. Usually, the child is left to grow up and become subjected to numerous pressures about him, until somewhere along in his adolescence, he becomes imbued with some idea that he would wish to become something or another. Now, this may be well and good to a certain extent, but we must remember that sometimes a child has been influenced by a psychic memory or an impingement from some previous lifetime. The child, in expressing such vocational aptitudes or desires is, in a sense of the word, merely wishing to work out a karmic condition which he may have incurred in a previous lifetime. Or, as I have said, he may be falsely pressured into adopting some vocation which he is entirely unsuited for and one in which he will quite likely waste a considerable portion of his life vainly trying to orient himself into performing and which will later become a very odious profession.

In many other planets the system of analyzing the characteristics and potentials of the child is begun soon after birth, so that the educational systems into which he enters, and to which he is subjected will be of such nature wherein the child is made fully cognizant of the direction of life which he is taking. He will not be pressured into this system, but rather, it will be very subtly interjected into his life so that he will become infused and completely embody the fulfilling a lifetime of such a vocation for which he is more suitably adapted. Should his aptitude be of such nature that training shall be entered into, wherein there are no particular propensities or outstanding characteristics in the child's nature, he is still, however, quite likely to be made a very capable and efficient citizen of his community through such vocational and directional aptitude guidance that he will, in his future days and evolutions, be much more constructively minded and much more developed and a more active participant in the community life about him.

The idea of colleges and universities, as they exist today, is very firmly entrenched in part, in the traditional aspects of learning as have existed with the inception or since the first days of such origins of these institutions.

Likewise, great emphasis is given to the sporting activities which have sometimes caused considerable derelictions with the student and his participation in the curricular activities of the institution where he is trying to obtain some sort of a degree of learning. So, all in all, the idea of vocational guidance being left until the more fully developed teen age, or until the adulthood years, is one which should be very strongly and emphatically rectified, so that the child can be entered as a mere youngster into such vocational guidance as will more suitably fit him for the life which he is to live. There was a closer adherence to this principle even in the so-called 'dark ages' wherein many youngsters were entered into periods of apprenticeship.

If you remember, in studying the histories of that time, there were in existence rather large systems of guilds or craftsmen throughout not only the European but through the Asiatic countries as well. Almost everyone was trained in some sort of craft or in some kind of trade; even the ladies were very deft in spinning and weaving, and in sewing and numerous other activities of their daily lives. The kings and queens were no exception. Usually, the period of apprenticeship was entered into at a very early age, sometimes at even the tender age of six or eight years, so that the child usually spent ten or fifteen years in the apprenticeship of the master-craftsman.

However, the austerities of such apprenticeship would not appeal to the youngster of your present day and age who has been reared in luxury which would be the envy of any king or emperor a hundred years or so ago. We could not imagine any youngster who has been pampered and living in a civilized age and time such as in your day of automobiles, with hot and cold water, plumbing and numerous civilized conveniences, as being likely to arise at five or six on a cold wintry morning to blow the coals of an open fireplace, to help prepare the breakfast meal and sweep and clean the house in preparation for the new tasks of the day which would probably involve him for at least twelve or fourteen hours. To such a youngster of your present day and age, this sort of apprenticeship would mean nothing more or less than pure slavery and such a condition he could not possibly tolerate.

Now I see that you have become accustomed — as you have been noting, seated in the park-like area immediately before one of the thirty-three entrances of this huge Temple — to the pulsating beauty of this dimension. We shall arise and walk up the seven steps which lead to this first entrance. Before going in, however, it would be quite obvious to you that it would be impossible, in one book or in one lifetime, to give you a very adequate and full description or exploration of the other remaining thirty two sections of this great Center. I shall, however merely sum this up in a general way by saying that they are, academically, rather largely devoted to the different periods of history, and in the transition of the historical pageants as they have existed on the earth from time to time. To explore each one of these sections would be, to the average student, something rather repetitious in nature, as much of the contents of these huge sections are very historical in nature, and relate to the different epochs of time in which man has lived on the earth planets as well as numerous other planets with which we are associated. We have purposely avoided entering into the discussion or description of any other planet as this would only tend to confuse the student of Truth. So that, all in all, as you have been given a portion of a factual exploration into one of the Centers, we will say that the remaining thirty-two are to a degree, the same nature; and that in these sections you will find numerous students and, in some cases in certain portions of one or another of the sections, you would find large groups of students, small or growing children who had passed from earth or from some other terrestrial planet, possibly before they had completed their full reincarnation. There are numerous 'differences in the interpretations of the periods of reincarnations within every individual, and sometimes it is quite obvious to see that the full completion or cycle is sometimes terminated before it is fully expressed into some dimension. It therefore, remains for the individual to reinstate himself in his purpose and to his own intent, and to further complete such a cycle in a suitable dimension, otherwise, this too, would induce some sort of karma to the individual as he is trying to work these things out which are impeding his progress.

Now, let us pass directly through this doorway, as you are somewhat amazed to find yourself standing somewhere in the middle of a huge bowl-shaped area, something like a coliseum or a sporting stadium in your own earth dimension. The differences here, however, are quite apparent in the nature and in the structure of the building itself. As you look about you, there are the crystalline structures with which you have become so familiar; and looking up and down into the various tiers and rows of seats, you can well imagine that this huge temple could hold at least two or three hundred thousand people. I could remind you that this is not necessarily a temple which is stable in size, but could be enlarged if some such future event were to take place wherein it would be necessary for a million or so persons to enter into this temple, and it could be enlarged in a very brief period of time to accommodate this very vast number of people who would enter in and be seated within these confines.

Overhead, if you will notice, there is a huge vaulted dome that seems to be transparent in nature; transparent with the exception of the large circular section which contains the thirty-three lenses or discs which are many feet in diameter. Looking down into the center of this large bowl-like depression, you will see a huge circular stage or platform, which is, within itself, about three or four hundred feet in diameter and rests upon a series of steps. You will see also, that the surface of this huge platform or stage is divided into thirty-three sections, each one of a different color or nature. There is, on the outer rim of each of these sections, a periphery of pure crystal, and on top of the surface of each crystal, there is a large flame which seems to be glowing, yet is steady — something like the flame of a candle. However, this flame would be about six feet tall and is of a pure white radiant nature. There is, also, immediately behind each one of these cubes and flames a raised dias where there is a seat. In the ceremony which is to take place within a few days, there will be the thirty-three representatives from the thirty-three Logi who will come into this Temple. They will be seated in their respective positions, each one upon His own raised dias or His own section of the platform, for the purpose of the ceremony.

Within the center of the semi-circle is also a section which has twelve different divisions wherein will be seated the Council of Twelve. The center section itself will be immediately devoted to the Master of the entire Shamballas who is, at the present time, the man who was formerly known on your earth as Jesus; or, rather to avoid confusion, let us say that this is the man and His polarity who are perfectly merged for this occasion; and in their merging they will assume their pure dimensional relationship with the whole integrated concept of the biune division, as has been explained to you in previous

1058

discussions.

This observance which will take place will be in a corresponding period of the twenty-first day of December in your Gregorian calendar. This is for the purpose of projecting at that time, intense radiations of Celestial Energies into the terrestrial dimension of the earth; and, as you see immediately above, each flame is glowing upon this cube-like altar; there is, in the ceiling above it in the huge dome, a corresponding huge lense which is focusing a pure beam of energy directly upon the flame. These flames are never allowed to die, but remain motionless and perpetual and serve numerous functions and different initiation ceremonies wherein the initiate comes to the Center to study. He must, of course, by nature, enter into such initiations as will immediately process him into the dimension in which he is to either serve or to be so tutored. I will not, at this time, promise that you will be here when this particular ceremony takes place, as this will be dependent, in part, upon conditions of a physical nature in the world about you; however, we will do our utmost if you so desire to witness this ceremony, and if it can be done without any danger to yourself, we shall be most happy to assist you in witnessing it. It must be borne in mind, however, that there will be tremendous energies in force and in play, during this ceremony, and we would have to set up certain shielding and protective devices which would insulate you from incurring some damage into the psychic centers of your body. However, we shall wait and see what comes forth during the next day or so.

So, now, if you will cast your eyes about, look upon the beauty about you, and into the great vaulted canopy or dome to the huge dimension of the temple which is immediately before you. In a very short time this will be filled to almost overflowing with numerous souls who have migrated here from the various other centers and astral worlds to witness the Christmas festival. These people are all, in themselves, related in their different transitions and in their different migrations; they have, at some time, been connected with the terrestrial planet earth and they are, therefore, quite interested in taking part in these observances in a pure spiritual nature. There will be no gift wrapping or packaging at this time. Rather, there will be an exchange of a gift which is of much greater value to mankind in general. This is the gift of the projection of pure brotherly love, to the peace of mind and security, and in the knowledge and in the knowing that each individual is, himself, an integrated part of the concept of God; that he is immortal and imperishable; that he is, by his own right and jurisdiction, as a child of God, so imbued with God-like qualities and virtues that he, too, in his future evolutions can become God-like in nature. So, until we can be together again, dear ones, with all our love and our most heart-felt projections of positive rays and energies, we remain, your brothers and sisters.

— Eliason.

(I, Ruth, asked here, if this ceremony was the same one of which a certain mystic spoke of seeing, and this was the answer: "My dear one, there are many orders and factions of a spiritual nature which are interjected into the earth dimensions at the Christmas time. The order to which you refer is one in which a large group of many thousands of different individuals known as monks, priests, and other so-called holy men, who have lived upon the earth at different times, make a particular point of having this procession at Easter time. They come from different planes of Shamballa, and from some of the higher astral worlds; through the quickening of spirit, as at Christmas time, it enables them to make close contact. They can literally weave great bands of spiritual energy about the aura of the earth and into the minds and hearts of individuals. This is all part of the ceremonies which originate from the Shamballas. However, they are brought into close contact with the earth in a more personal relationship through these different, more spiritual men and women who had lived upon the earth at different times. Part of the ceremony will be led by such personages as Mother Cabrini, Saint Francis of Assisi, and many other individuals of such nature. I do hope this has been cleared up for you.'')

CHAPTER XCIV

Greetings Dear Ones, and a most heartfelt and positive wish for your happiness and well-being over the coming Christmas holidays. My identity was, formerly, on the earth, known in the Egyptian period as Hermes, and later in the Grecian or Hellenic period as Plato. I am momentarily forsaking my seat in the Council in the Temple to conduct you in the final and concluding transmissions from this Center. In the coming several months, the final chapters of the series of books will be given to you from the two remaining sections and will conclude in a grand and final climax on the Easter festival. At that time the great Leader Himself will give a Message. Now, a word of preparation before we enter the Temple where you are to witness the ceremony of the torch lighting which takes place during the mid-winter solstice; it is one of interest, not only to the planet earth, but to a number of other terrestrial planets in the great universe. Primarily, the people who are in the temple at this time are those who, at different times, have had a period or reincarnations of earth life, and they are all quite naturally very much interested in becoming an active participant which enables them to do some small or individual part in projecting some intensities and rays of love to their fellow man in the lower dimensions.

As there is a great amount of power within this temple, we have prepared something very special for you. As you see before you, there is something which looks like a large, beautiful iridescent soap bubble. It is actually a sphere of radiant energy which we have constructed and with which we have endowed or imbued certain properties. You will step through just as you would through a real soap bubble; however, this bubble will not break. Now, that you have stepped through, you find yourself in the immediate inside diameter of the bubble and the great Center here in this parkway has seemingly lost some of its brilliance. The walls of the 'bubble' as they are somewhat like glass, have properties which are like the sun-glasses used by different terrestrial people to cut down the glare of solar energies. This bubble, also has peculiar refractionary properties, and now you will be able to see through the aura of some of the more advanced individuals whom you will see in the Central Section of the Temple in the ceremony which is soon to begin.

If you remember in the transmission where you saw Serapis giving a discussion from a stone altar in the center of the lake, and if you had been in this soap bubble at that time, (I am calling it a soap bubble!), you would have been able to see more of the inside of the actual individual form of this person. The properties of refraction which are so contained, will be in direct proportion to the degree of concept which your present status of life has thus oriented you to being able to perceive an individual as somewhat of the form and shape in which you might naturally or normally expect a person to so appear.

Were the earth man to view these Higher Beings, he would conceive them to appear much like himself rather than as they do exist in their true perspectives and dimensional characteristics. However, for your own status of evolution and advancement, your mind has been so conditioned that you can perceive them as they so exist and, thus, they will appear to you through the walls of this energy bubble. Now, let us proceed directly to the high balcony which overlooks the huge bowl of the Central Temple. In the previous discussion it was described as something which resembled the athletic stadiums of the earth at your time except that it was tremendously enlarged and absolutely circular in fashion. We can look down from our position over the heads of thousands of individuals directly onto the great central platform. The people whom you see about you are very much interested in the ceremony just as yourself; and while you see that the distance is very great, they are not concerned with the factors of such relationship which might limit physical eyes. Their vision is so perfect that they can see just as closely as they wish from whatever particular position they occupy in this huge Central Temple.

Looking down directly into the great center platform, you see what appears to be several concentric or radial rings of beautiful glowing individuals. Peering through the walls of your bubble, you can visualize, through the radiant aura which they are projecting, the actual Being or form of the individual. In most cases they are not one individual, but two, as they are perfectly merged with their biune or biocentric counterpart. This is a peculiar and rather difficult abstract concept for the average individual to master. These two individuals are now perfectly balanced and in perfect cooperation and in perfect harmony with each other, however, they can extend outwardly, just as you are doing through the astral body into whatever dimension they may assume which may be entirely different from each other. I am referring of course to those who are called the Logi or the Archangels and to the more Advanced Individuals who are assembled here for the purpose of this ceremony at this time.

The exact placement of the rings of individuals, as you see, was partially described to you previously. There is one very large ring which seats through several rows, a large number of people who are attired in a rather striking blue radiant garment which has been especially prepared and adapted for this time. These are the more active participants in the ceremony and each carries a long wand which is something like a conductor's baton in a modern orchestra. It is, of course, composed of the familiar beautiful energy from which all things here are constructed. Within this circle are also many of the Teachers and more Advanced Individuals who are working in the Seven Centers of the Shamballas, not only as teachers but sometimes as students. Now, there is a separation of some distance to the next ring. Here, you will see that there are thirty-three different sections or separations, wherein several individuals are seated. These are the Lords or the Logi who come from the offices of the Seven Celestial Kingdoms. They are, in the terms of the earth language, the Liaison branches of the Celestial Government or Kingdoms which relate in their own official capacities, not only to the Shamballas, but also in a spiritual way, to the more advanced spiritual inceptions into the terrestrial dimensions. I might mention a few of them which would somewhat acquaint you with the nature of these individuals. Looking off to the right you will see two persons seated in one section of the ring who were formerly known on the earth as Elisha and Elijah. Over to the left there are two other Individuals who are known as Gabriel and Maroni. Down in the center section of this ring is another shining and illuminous Personage who is known as Matrea. You will notice also, that there is something else that is peculiar about this assemblage, they are facing the center of the ring and not with their faces toward the audience as might be supposed in the normal function of some of the earth ceremonies. There is a definite reason for this as you will soon see. Now, there is another separation wherein there exists another concentric ring of individuals who are called the 'Council of Twelve', and this ring is divided into twelve different sections wherein the leading Lord or Master of this Council so resides and officiates.

To name a few of these individuals, I would name some who have been previously mentioned such as Zoroaster, Buddha, Krishna, Osiris, Mohammed, etc.

In the exact center of this Council of Twelve is the individual who was once known upon the earth as the man Jesus, and who acquainted Himself with you as 'Shattock', from the mother planet Venus at one time. Now that you have, in a way, become acquainted with the general formation of this ceremony we will see that it is about to begin. The hundreds of thousands of individuals will first begin by chanting a certain song which is the familiar song of the energies which you have heard before. This song, however, seems to have some peculiar significance, or that it reminds you of some of the Christmas carols which you have heard upon the earth. This song seems to lift and rise and fall in cadence and, as it does so, there are wonderful and beautiful waves of etheric energy of numerous colors which are cascading down into the central platform. We see, also, that there has been a gradual increase in activity in the central section. I am not referring to physical activity but to the projection of the Celestial Energies or the God Forces from the Minds of these Illumined Souls and Archangels who are thus assembled. These energies all seem to be projecting and focusing into the exact center of this platform and onto the Individual who is known as Jesus. These energies are further fortified and strengthened by the huge prismatic lenses from the ceiling above from the great domes which are so focused that they, too, are lending and aiding the energies which are being projected to this Master. He is holding out his hands in a form and a way in which there seems to be a round luminous ball of intense Radiant Energies which are being gradually built upon the surface of His hands. This ball of energy would be several feet in diameter in measurement of your earth dimension. It is a tremendously pulsating, throbbing energy form which is so exceedingly bright that your eyes, even through your glass canopy, are somewhat blinded by the intense radiance of this ball of energy.

Now, the cascading song from the hundreds of thousands of minds rises and falls in increased intensity. The individuals or Logi in the great section have now arisen and are standing; gradually, they are drawing away into such a form which will present a large pathway up toward the center of the enclosure where the Master Jesus is standing. Now, the outer ring of individuals, who are dressed in the intense blue garments, are forming in a certain line. They are holding aloft their long wands of energy. They begin to file singly one by one closely together, toward the central figure in the great center enclosure. As they approach Him they hold out their wands and touch the luminous ball of fire which is being held by His hands and immediately the tip of the wands glow with an intense starlike brilliance; so, they pass on and a new person steps up and touches his wand upon the ball of fire on and on. Actually, there will be several hundred or more of these individuals who will touch their wands upon this ball of fire, or there may be several thousand. When the ceremony is completed, the large ball is in no wise depleted but forms and ascends on up through the central temple dome and is dissipated into the great Celestial void about the temple.

Now, these individuals, who have lighted their wands, will descend unto the aura of the earth where, in the next several days, they will encircle the earth seven times. Then they will descend as spiritual beings, invisible to mankind, and mingle with the countless millions of people upon the surface of the earth. There, as they walk about through the crowds, they will find those persons who have been touched with the Christmas spirit and as this is the time when, sometimes even sinners are made saints, it is thus because this light will touch the hearts of the individuals who have become infused and imbued with the spirit of Christmas. The spirit of well-being and brotherly love which wells up within the hearts and minds of mankind over the surface of the terrestrial earth is not one of mere happenstance which might be called preconditioned psychological impact, but it is a direct derivation of a combination of astrophysical elements. The earth, in passing through the great magnetic lines of the universe so meets and joins these lines at the Winter Solstice, and, during this period, it is so that there is a quickening of the spirit, and, thus, the Saints who are mingling among the earth people with their wands are touching the minds and hearts of those individuals who have felt and who are realizing the spiritual quickening of these great magnetic lines of force or energy.

The individuals with the wands, themselves, are former dwellers upon the terrestrial earth. They could be named by the hundreds of holy men and women who have come and gone among the races of mankind and who have left behind them the blessings of their Illumined and expanded consciousness. They are the monks, the nuns, the workers who have come and gone, some unnoticed and unherald, some who have not left their names as luminous marks upon the pages of history, but nonetheless, they, too, had their own spiritual transitions upon the earth, and the earth was made richer by their having mingled with its peoples. I might name many of these luminous personages who have lived upon the earth and who are now about to go into the aura of the earth and mingle with the people. Such personages as St. Frances of Assisi, Mother Cabrini, Florence Nightingale, and of course there are a host of others which would take too long and be too tiring to pursue. However, rest assured that each one comes with His magic wand with its star upon it so this star becomes an individual 'Star of Bethlehem' to each individual upon the earth who has so quickened and is so reliving the spiritual consciousness of the transition.

The story of the Messiah in the Christian religion is

not alone among the stories of the creation of Avatars or of the Bringer of Saints among the races of the people; and all nations, all creeds must have their own personal Savior. So, it is in Islam with the prophet Mohammed, so it is in India with Buddha, in China with Confucius, and in Egypt and other countries of the world as well. Thus, it has been that the beneficent God, who has provided all things has also provided these sparks of Light and illuminous qualities of man's spiritual nature which comes from within himself.

And so, dear ones, remember that at your awakening on Christmas morning, and in your consciousness of the Christ Light and the personal 'Savior' within you, that perhaps one of these Illumined Persons may have come to you and touched your mind and your heart with the 'Star of Bethlehem'; and that you, too, have had the quickening and the awakening of the spirit, not because of a vision which happened two thousand years ago, but one which happens to you each year; one which happens to you each time you attune yourself unto the Light that It may be brought unto you; thus, it will be and so it will always remain so, for the Supreme Consciousness of the Immortal Creator has placed all things within the reach of every man. No man needs to depend upon another for his own salvation; neither does he have to cry aloud in the wilderness and in the despair of his own emotional consequences. He must always know and realize that the personal image of God within himself has supplied his every need and has fulfilled his every wish, and his innermost desires; and that only in living apart from this consciousness, does he become profane and defile this concept of the Supreme Consciousness and the Christ Light which is within himself.

So dear ones, in the days to come, learn to love one another. Learn to realize the fullest measure of the benefit of this all-wise and all-knowing and most beneficent Intelligence which has so conceived and constructed the mighty universes; yea, and even every blade of grass which you trod upon with your feet. The mystery of creation and nature, in itself, in its most profound and abstract concept should be one of constant creative inspiration to each and every one of you; and that you should dwell in the house of the Infinite forever.

So be it.

THE

VOICE OF UNARIUS

Clairvoyantly Received

By

Ernest L. Norman

***

The Sixth Volume of

THE PULSE OF CREATION

***

*

Published by

Unarius - Science of Life

CHAPTER XCV

Good evening. We are so happy to renew our contact since our previous transmission which unfortunately was not recorded (something went wrong with the mechanism of the recorder) however, as you said, dear sister, a while ago that naught is lost. This is Morya, and my brother Kuthumi will conduct you in your next explorations into the number one section of Shamballa which is called Panthorius. We have also named these cities and the Centers of this great planet in honor of the new movement which you are at the present opening into the terrestrial planet earth; so it is, therefore, that we dedicate the new name of 'Unarius' to this central city which is dedicated to leadership.

Now, however, before you are taken to the planet and while you are resting somewhere in midspace in the astral form, we will take up the problem of leadership as an explanation to the various persons who may, in the future, read these transcripts. One of the books by a disciple upon the planet earth has depicted the first Center of Shamballa as being under the symbology of a mallet which is being held in the hand. This we would like to change. There is nothing forceful in leadership, and primarily all leadership, as is taught from Shamballa or any section of the Shamballas is rather conducted purely from the inward self from the Spiritual Consciousness. We do not teach the leadership of the armies or such types of leadership which lead to death and destruction. This type of leadership is taught by the organizations of the black forces which are far removed, fortunately, from the spiritual Centers of Shamballa.

For your new symbol for Unarius and for the planet of Panthorius and the new city of Unarius, you may have the symbol of the heart as it is depicted in your earth art literature. In the center of the heart will be a block or a

1071

square of pure crystal and upon the center will be the flame of life; surrounding this heart shall be a golden circle. This will be the symbol of Unarius which speaks that it is leadership from the flame of life to the heart or the inner consciousness and surrounded by the infinite magnitude of God's Infinite Wisdom.

Now, we see that you are hovering over a very beautiful planet something of a brilliant orange hue, and coming closer you are reminded mentally of your visit to Mars except that this planet is much more brilliant and of a pulsating or glowing character which distinguishes it from any material planet. Coming down, directly you see we have landed in front of what apparently appears to be a huge mountain that is seemingly covered with a beautiful city. The plane upon which you are standing, as you look closely, is actually a brilliantly colored mosaic tile courtyard which extends for a space of about three or four earth miles all around the base of this mountain. Looking at the huge mountain which is of the purest amber crystal, you see that there are seven exactly spaced concentric rings or levels around the entire surface of the mountain. They seem to be literally carved from this pure crystal amber mountain which is of such radiance and intensity that it almost blinds the eyes.

Upon each of these seven levels, or rather six levels and a flat top, you see stretching out the numerous buildings, dormitories, and other structures wherein are living at the present time, those persons who are teaching or are being taught. Also, you will see huge parkways wherein are displayed the most fantastic floral gardens which you could possibly imagine. You might wander for days through these numerous parkways on the different levels and never actually see anything that would be similar to any other parkway you have previously visited. All in all, it is a very beautiful place which defies description. All of the glowing buildings are made of the same structural crystal-like energy in a multitude and a variety of colors ranging from the deep purple to the purest white — colors which, as you see, seem to suit the personal vibration of many of the persons who are passing through or dwelling within.

A little more explanation of the actual function of this beautiful city in what is called spiritual leadership, or leadership in any other form would be quite in order at this moment. So, we shall pause here at the foot of one of these great terraces before we ascend. Each terrace is related to its own particular other Center of Shamballa as you have previously explored them. Thinking for just a moment, you will see that there is a definite relationship in the function of this great city, as the graduates from one or more of the other Centers will come here before reincarnating to the earth where they can learn how to use the knowledge they have acquired in a directed fashion. This is the leadership which we teach. Most people are quite incapable of leadership, and although they may possess all of the necessary brains and qualifications, there is something, a mysterious quality, which they seem to lack. On your earth plane you have often wondered, perhaps, at the seeming mystery which always surrounds some particular individual who seems, at the proper moment, in some critical situation whether it is governmental in nature or concerns the progress of a community, a group of people, or in an infinite number or variety of such expressions, to suddenly rise, head and shoulders above the crowd and everyone turns to this person. It seems as if a sort of electric current or a magnetic flux courses through the people and they turn to this person with confidence to lead them through a crisis. This is the quality of leadership which the various individuals have expressed in numerous dimensional concepts throughout your own planet as well as in the numerous other planets wherein man will dwell; this, naturally can be assumed to exist in the higher and the lower spiritual planets as well as on the terrestrial planets.

The actual qualities of spiritual leadership extend into many different planes of expression; whether they are the qualifications which enable a school teacher to teach a group of students or whether the person is a great political leader who will lead a nation through many critical periods of development and growth, it is all one and the same. All of these individuals have learned of the existence of this spiritual leadership and how to direct this leadership into the channels of their own minds. The exact process of this type of mental transference is an extension of the principle of psychokinesis, or psychokinetics as you may know it. It too, as a principle, resides in a dimension of an extended sense of clairvoyance. It is a feeling of Infinity and an affinity with the mental powers of the person who has assumed the leadership. Your history books would explain to you the innumerable types of leadership which seem to spring from the inner spiritual nature of some individual whether he is a great composer, an artist, a philosopher or perhaps a priest or a physician who has dedicated his life to the service of humanity. In whatever capacity this person finds himself, his measure of success in leadership will depend upon how well he has learned to project the powers and directive forces of his inner mind to the channels of inward perception or the organs of clairvoyance in every individual.

Now, looking upward again into this huge expansive crystal city before you, there seem to shoot out into space numerous bright orange colored hues and rays; there seem to be coming to it and going from it in all directions, numerous specks of light which I perceive in your inner consciousness and this pleases me greatly for now you are actually perceiving these persons in spiritual flight as they pass from Center to Center.

The plateaus of the great cities, as they are laid out in terraces, each in a succeeding rise or elevation are, as I have said, numbered and are vibrating or linked to some other Center of Shamballa on their own particular frequency rate or, as it has been called in your earth language, a ray. The top, or the Seventh Plane of this whole structure ends in a huge temple of such vast and magnificent proportions that it eclipses even some of the larger temples such as you saw in Aurelius. These concepts are as you see, staggering and beyond your imagination or conception, as they deal with the services of mankind in their respective positions to even hundreds of millions of people who are coming and going. Like Parhelion, this Number One Center, or the plane of leadership, is actually the pivot point, or the point wherein all the other seven planes link themselves and revolve and oscillate in a sort of frequency relationship in their various functional orders.

To philosophize for a moment: all knowledge or wisdom as it is incurred by the individual here is quite useless unless it is directed to the earth minds and directed to those earth scientists, or to those in some position of righteous or even false authority in their respective expression in the different dimensions which is called parapsychology, for these people know comparatively little or nothing of this interdimensional concept. To peer beyond the veil of mortality would be to engulf the reactionary minds of most individuals with the vast magnitude of mental intercourse which is going on not only between peoples of the earth but between the peoples of the hundreds of thousands of other terrestrial and astral worlds and planets. In fact, it is quite safe to say, for the benefit of the savants who are trying to delve into these inner mysteries of man's life upon the earth, that your daily social functions in the structures of civilization as they now exist — just as they have also done in the past countless ages of the history of your earth — would have been quite impossible had they not existed on levels of what is called mental telepathy or the interchange of idea, thought form, and consciousness from individual to individual or collectively into the masses of humanity as a whole.

The average individual in a terrestrial dimension who has so concerned himself in the reactionary thought processes of his own planet in his own dimension at his own time, would be quite startled to learn that he is never alone; that his thoughts are open books and are turned page by page by those who know the simple process of frequency relationship and, as he thinks, he literally tunes himself in and out to countless hundreds of thousands or even millions of minds who are thus blinking off and on like an infinite number or series of tiny little lights which seem to bob up and down through the countless limitless miles of the great universe. These little lights all synchronize themselves as tiny vibrations of thought forms or energies which are pulsating back and forth within their own orbital frequencies; thus no man is ever alone with his thoughts. The objective should be to 'suspend' conscious, reactive thinking! As the young man explained it on your TV apparatus, to think of nothing, and to direct one's consciousness inwardly, one becomes a part of this vast pulsating sea of twinkling lights which we have symbolized as the energies of man's mentality of millions of souls who are in tune with him in the innumerable dimensions throughout the vastness of God's countless and Celestial Universes.

Now, I fear I have digressed somewhat from our true course and purpose; however, some philosophy must be interjected at different times, as this is primarily the life blood or purpose of the whole series of explorations and transmissions. This must be done and duly constituted; otherwise, the burdens of man could not be lifted to such a degree that he would be able to crawl from under his great burden or load of iniquities and again stand upright and face the Light of The Infinite. The various plateaus or elevations are quite obviously of such a vast extent that it would be quite safe to say that you could spend something of a period equivalent to a thousand years of your earth life in going around the entire circumference of these different plateaus or elevations, and you would, indeed, have to walk rapidly to look into the various buildings to obtain a sense of evaluation of their functions. It is, therefore, impossible to give you anything more than a superficial or, as someone there around you might say, a 'thumbnail' description or exploration into these Centers. We hope also this will be something which will tempt the individual in the future evolutions in his flight through space, as he calls it, to pause momentarily for a 'few thousand years' or so in our great city of Unarius on the planet of Panthorius and, if he does, we will indeed welcome him.

Numbering these great plateaus from the bottom to the top, we would say that the true city or the Number One Section is the plateau of Leadership. The Second, Third, Fourth, Fifth, and Sixth all correspond to the same successive numbers of sections of Shamballa. The Seventh, of course, corresponds to the Seventh plane, which also links it into another certain fashion with the great Center of Parhelion. These things are, in their own way, explained through the principles of frequency or harmonic vibration in your nomenclature of the earth scientist.

Now, we have ascended into the first plateau which is the one of leadership. Here, rapidly skirting around through the various buildings and great dormitories, we see that if we enter some of these huge buildings, we will find people very busily engaged in numerous different dimensions of endeavor, which will teach them something of the histories of the various terrestrial and cosmic planets throughout the universe. You will see, also, that there are, as in other Centers, great museums which factually portray the mysteries of these people. There is also a considerable amount of scientific apparatus in some of these Centers which demonstrates to the student, in the higher brackets of the electronic sciences, how the various wave forms of mind energy can be collected and projected, how it is that the student can develop the necessary qualifications which enable him to send out these certain magnetic impulses into the minds of his fellow man, which will cause him to lean upon or depend upon him for some type of this leadership. Also he will learn something of the differences between this type of spiritual, inward, constructive leadership and that leadership which has led armies of nations against each other and which has decimated great cities and left the bodies of the populations therein strewn about for food for the vultures.

However, we shall not defile our thoughts one moment by the evil consequence of these black forces which have so destructively, at different times, led mankind astray. Here, you will also see mothers or, shall we say, women who are to become earth mothers to large families and they, too, develop a certain type of leadership which will enable them to raise their brood of youngsters; and should they progress, they may reach such a point that they may bring into the world some youngster who will have been a student who had studied here in this Center. This, in itself, is something which can give rise to many thought-provoking questions. You may look about you into the faces of your relatives, your friends and your neighbors, and you may at some time see a fellow student whom you have been with in one of the Centers of Shamballa. But for the present moment, Kuthumi and I convey to you the love vibrations of the countless millions of souls in these different Centers. Until our next exploration.

— Morya.

CHAPTER XCVI

Dear friends, I am most happy to serve you. I was formerly upon the earth plane about two or three hundred years after the advent of the teacher Buddha and was known as Asoka. I was very fortunate to be able, in my position as a prince and a king, to spread this very worthy philosophy and doctrine throughout the fair land of India. You are quite right in saying that present day versions of the old religions of the past do not, in many ways, resemble those simple truths which were taught by these higher Masters or Avatars who appeared from time to time upon the earth. However, that has been discussed somewhat lengthily by other very worthy compatriots of these sections, so without further ado, we shall go directly to our Center Panthorius which we have called leadership or it might be called integration. On our previous visit you emerged, I believe, somewhere upon the ground before a huge building on the first plateau. Now, we had better describe these different plateaus to you so that you can factually relate them in their proper order and sequence as they relate to the other Centers, for it is important to learn this relationship.

As Morya told you, the individual learns to integrate and to bring into conscious focus the wisdom and knowledge which he has learned. Such wisdom would be useless without the proper means to spread this in some lower plane. Beginning with the first plateau, it is one in which is taught and learned the various necessary factors for types of political leadership used with the great masses of people on planets similar to the earth. We might mention one or two which would serve as examples of what we mean by such leadership. A recent American named Franklin D. Roosevelt, typifies this type of leadership and, though you might question the fact that he was a leader through a great world war, yet this leadership, in itself, was not necessarily learned, nor was it a direct expletory fact or expression from these higher Shamballas. There are numerous other leaders whom we could mention down through the periods of time in the nations of the world who would demonstrate a very high type of leadership. Your country has been led and guided by many of these more highly trained and developed leaders who obtain at least some knowledge from these Centers of Shamballa; George Washington and Abraham Lincoln could of course be numbered among these people.

In the past ages you may pick out many whom you know who could also be classified as such political leaders. You may also wonder why these people, in reincarnating into the earth as leaders, do not remember any of these experiences in the higher spiritual dimensions which we are presently exploring. And the reasons are very obvious. Such knowledge of their pre-existence would quite likely color or, shall we say, give them advantages over their fellow men which they would not understand. As in the case of any highly developed clairvoyant whom the masses do not understand, the people turn away their faces, make derisive remarks, yea, even destroy persons who display wisdom beyond the general dimension of wisdom which is expressed by the masses of the people.

The second plateau is directly integrated and linked to the Second Plane of Shamballa known as the plane of Education which you previously visited. Here it is, in the great dimension of these great buildings on this second plateau, you will find huge classrooms wherein are the various savants, professors or other teachers of the different sciences and theosophies, theologies, and philosophies of the earth and of many other planets similar to the earth. Here, too, you will find the same unified type of projection or focus which will enable the individuals to be outstanding in their own fields of endeavor.

The Third Plane is the one which is connected to the

section of Aurelius known as the plane of philosophy and synthesis. Here, again, this same leadership is focused and integrated. The Fourth Plane, as you remember, was Helianthus; the Fifth was a secondary counterpart of the over planet of Parhelion and links it with the scientific plane of integration. The Sixth Plane, too, is linked to the planet Venus which is spiritual healing, guidance, and psychotherapy in many ways and in many different realms and dimensions. The Seventh is one which you have not yet visited, and is linked to the temple which forms the apex of this huge Center. This is the plane of devotees or those persons who express ritualism and the more divine essence of the inner spiritual nature in a pure and, shall I say 'Angelic', relationship with higher dimensions of the God Consciousness.

Perhaps at this moment we might peer into one of the nearby buildings which is before us and, as we do so, we will see students who are grouped about; here is one particular group which we shall look upon for a moment while I explain what is taking place. As you see, there are a number of students grouped immediately back of the one individual who is seated in a special kind of chair; he has passed into a deep meditative state of absolute inner silence while his brothers about him are concentrating and learning to use and to focus their minds into his, into such directive channels as would be quite similar to the conditions which will be met in the terrestrial dimensions when this individual, who is seated in the chair, shall find himself in the physical body. He will thus be separated quite widely in a frequency relationship from his fellow brothers who are standing there with him so that consequently, they will have to be quite adept at focusing and sending him the thought projections and the rays of wisdom and thoughts which will be necessary for him in his inspirational work in his earth life.

A typical example of what could happen here could be

1081

visualized as one of the composers whose birthday, after several hundred years, was observed; we are referring to Wolfgang Mozart. If you follow his history closely, you will see that at the age of four he composed different types of piano and string ensemble music; and at the age of six, he gave a joint recital with his sister, and before he was eight had composed his first symphony. It is also said of Mozart that he composed three symphonies in less than eight weeks' time toward the close of his earth life. Now, you see there must have been some spiritual integration here with this person even when he was a very small child, which enabled him to perform these prodigious demonstrations of mentality and he was called a genius. However, it can be said that Mozart spent considerable time in Coralanthus before he emerged into the corresponding section in this dimension where he learned with his fellow students and formed the necessary elements of integration which enabled him to bring this music into the world.

The same pattern of integration follows through in whatever particular facet of life the individual is portraying, providing, of course, that he is an outstanding personality and one who is worthy of special consideration. There are vast numbers and countless millions of people on the earth in your day who do not have even the most rudimentary or fragmentary knowledge of such spiritual integration. They act and react according to certain basic elemental orders of frequency relationship with their own psychic selves. Such men and women are indeed in a comparatively low state of evolution. It is fortunate, indeed, that man is sometimes inspired to live above these levels which are just a step removed from the elevation of animal expression, and I am most fortunate to be in such a position as to assist many of my fellow students and direct them into suitable channels which will enable them to further integrate their work on some earth plane.

You will see passing to and from these numerous buildings and classrooms in this Center on this particular plateau, people of such nature as shall, in the future hundreds of years of earth history, become most outstanding and who will leave a mark and an indelible impression on the history of the earth — worthwhile individuals who shall so worthily serve their fellow man in some form of leadership. Incidentally, in planes like this, many individuals who have lived or expressed more of the destructive tendencies in their earth lives are learning that in their service to mankind they are wiping out the black stains of their karmic past, thus enabling them to rebuild certain spiritual structures or spiritual bodies within themselves which will enable them to progress into higher dimensions of relationship.

In future explorations and chapters which relate to this section, we shall explain more fully to you what we believe is an important fact about which you should know; this is the actual construction of the pure superconscious self which is sometimes called your soul. We have noticed that the question of what the soul is, has become an important one in your minds at different intervals; and as you are progressing in the outside world in the activities of teaching, we shall factually explain to you the (so-called) soul as it exists. Although it may be in an abstract form and a bit difficult to understand, we hope that it will shed light upon the situation. Now, until such future time, as one of my Brothers shall resume and take you into another plateau of exploration, we shall temporarily suspend our operations.

— Asoka.

CHAPTER XCVII

Greetings, dear ones. I am so happy to come to you. I was known to you on the earth as Saint Teresa and was most happy that you, sister, recognized me by the fragrance, although I smiled about the 'lacy' description! It was Djwal Kul, who was supposed to give this transmission, but he is a true gentleman and bowed aside so that I might be able to come in. I am very much overwhelmed with the great spiritual power and the intensity of all these happenings that are going on around and about; but I will try to conduct you through this Second Section of this Center which is called 'Unarius'.

Now that you have arrived at the location of the second plane or plateau, many things have begun to be made more clear to you; and as your inner eye is becoming accustomed to the usual brilliant radiance with which we are surrounded, you see that you are standing in front of a temple here on this second elevation. You have also begun to notice, in the complete circumference of these planes or plateaus, there are seven different temples spaced at regular intervals. Before we describe why this is so, however, let us resume somewhat and review our previous exploration into the First Section which was the plane of integration.

It was on this first plateau or level, as was pointed out to you, that the student, initiate, or adept concluded his various and numerous studies in the different dimensions of Unarius (I must become used to this new name), but he came to this first center section and thus integrated or correlated in an objective way the dimensions of his mind, to learn just how to use this marvelous and wonderful wisdom which he had gained in going through these different sections. This you may call, for want of a better name, psychokinetics or the projection of the mind forces. In the second section which we are about to explore, I personally am one of the natives who has lived here for some time, as at one time, I was fortunate enough to serve as some sort of spiritual leader upon the earth plane. Since coming here, I have gained much more wisdom and knowledge which I hope will be useful to the service of mankind in some future day.

Now, dear ones, this section as you look into the various structures about you, relating you with their beautiful brilliance, you will see that it is of a different feeling or a different intensity than the one which you previously visited, with its deep radiant orange vibration, which is as near as we can describe such a condition as we do not have eyes in a physical sense. Here, the vibration might be termed as something which would impress you with a more saffron-like yellow or a pure radiant golden nature which relates you, in the understanding of a frequency relationship, with the Second Section of Unarius (formerly called Shamballa) which was devoted to education. It is here that such people come to complete and fulfill their specific destinies in the realm of teachings, as it will be expressed whether in some of the lower astral worlds or in some of the terrestrial worlds. It is through this Center that many of the most wonderful spiritual leaders who have appeared upon the earth plane have learned in some way to integrate their wisdom and teaching in such a manner that it will be most useful; or that perhaps it will be taught to people in the lower astral planes somewhere between here and the terrestrial earth whereby, in turn, it will be relayed to the earth people through the regular process of reincarnation.

I could mention quite a large number of people who have appeared upon your earth planet from time to time, who have assisted materially in freeing people from the various oppressive systems of materialism which they have built up around themselves through the wrong integration of life. Mostly, and for the largest part, we shall start with even the most humble of the teachers in the teaching profession, the little schoolmarm who sits behind her desk and teaches a small group of students, or the various priests or ministers who are somewhat more spiritually inclined in their natures into the different interpretations or dimensions of spiritual leadership, for it must not be inferred that all spiritual leaders, as they appear on your earth, are basically motivated by the higher principles of life, for some of them are very selfish and are completely frustrated in their lack of and need for the higher philosophy of life, and they are attempting to vindicate these inward suppressions upon their fellow men by giving the wrong interpretations into the various dimensions of spiritual knowledge.

However, you must all learn to discern for yourselves who are the wrong leaders and who are motivated by the higher spiritual principles of life, and, as Jesus pointed out, especially in your time there are many false teachers who are like ravenous wolves; even though they dress in sheep's clothing or in the robes of the ecclesiastical orders. Also we find much leadership of a much higher intelligent nature and of a more character-building propensity, even among the more humble walks of life in which there is no immediate association or any kind of leadership, either spiritual or otherwise; and these men and women portray such a strength of character that people inadvertently learn to lean upon them in moments of crisis wherein they may be given such spiritual healing and comfort that it will enable them to rise above their conditions.

We shall explore these beautiful buildings which you see about you and the temple itself; and I must explain these temples before the power begins to fade. Referring back somewhat to the concepts of how it is that we come and go into these different beautiful Centers of Unarius, we must all be somewhat conditioned within our spiritual bodies before we can enter and leave these places, because of the vibrations, as they are very harmonious in their overall relationship to each other; yet to gain the greatest benefit from the infusions of these Celestial Energies which are radiating and permeating in their own orbital frequencies, we must be conditioned or re-baptized, if you may call it so, into these various planes. This we do as you have seen by the different initiations, ceremonies, or processes which take place in these temples. Each temple around the circumference of each one of these planes, in itself, functions in what might be called a sub-harmonic frequency from any one of a number of the different planes or Centers so the student comes in at regular intervals when the ceremonies are held. He is conditioned by going through the different flames or the different rays, as they are centered or focused upon his being in the emergence, and during the various comings and goings of these people.

It is quite possible for us to come into any of these planes and stay there for just as long a period as we wish; however, we are something like the foreigner who comes from a distant country of Europe to your shores; he remains somewhat on the Ellis Island, I believe it is called, whereby he is somewhat conditioned and prepared. Further preparation and conditioning is necessary before he enters into the stratified concepts of your social life; and so it is here, except of course, that these things are not done in the material values, but are expressed in the higher rates and in the higher concepts of spiritual vibration. (Energy was ebbing, the Moderator's voice scarcely discernable, when suddenly an inflow of power became so strong that he could scarcely endure its intensity.) Yes, brother, I appreciate your feeling in your physical body. St. Francis of Assisi is standing here close to me; he wishes to project unto you some of the strength from the Radiant Energies which are stemming from the various Centers of his spiritual body and you should feel immediate change so we shall be enabled to proceed with transmission. (E.L.N. was renewed, as when a suffocating person was given oxygen – the sound or volume was instantly increased 200%.) There, you see that it is done; now we may proceed.

In walking around and through these various beautiful structures you will see that they are constructed, as before, of the same wonderful radiant energy which seems to come from everywhere. It is an energy or a substance which is like the very air that you breathe and it permeates and is absorbed into what you think is every portion of your body which, as you see, is actually your spiritual self. It does not look, in a pure sense, exactly like the bodies we have because it has not yet developed and resolved into the pure spiritual elements in which energy resides in these higher planes. However, do not feel let down nor should you deprecate yourself in any way, because these vibrations will, through the evolutions of time – and particularly in that time which is called death or the separation of the flesh – bring a new rebirth, and a re-entrance into a new higher spiritual dimension where your spiritual bodies or your psychic bodies, as you have called them, will take on the new hues and radiances which we here are seemingly radiating through our very beings. Because of the nature and intensity of these frequencies which are permeating into your spiritual body, we shall not attempt to keep you here with us too long, but shall return you to your own terrestrial dimension in a short time.

However, we would like to bring out a few more rather important facts before this particular exploration is terminated; these facts can be related much to your own particular expression of teaching into the minds of the people about you. This should be considered primarily a personal message of hope and inspiration; yet, we believe that it shall also serve a purpose to those people in the future who shall read these lines, for, as they, too, come into this consciousness of teaching and healing, they also, shall be inspired, even though there will be much to tend to discourage them and cause them despair. The elements of human conception or, as you have expressed it, as 'the threshold of perception', is to most people in your dominion and on your planet earth in a comparatively shadowy state. People simply lack a constructive way for personal analysis in the integration of the different factors of their own earth lives. They are like little children who wander about and play in the yard, and try out the numerous experiences which may or may not hurt them; but through the particular values of experience, they learn just what they must accept or reject.

Spiritual teaching is, shall I say, most subtle in its nature and does not appear as thunder clouds or as some stinging insect, or lightning bolt that may hurt or cause pain; but, rather, it is a subtle infusion of spiritual virtues of nature into the inner self which changes and diffuses the entire physical structures. It also changes the thinking processes and habits of people who come in contact with this most divine infusion of the Infinite Radiant Wisdom. Such changes may occur instantaneously; yet, very often the person who has had this change occur in him is not fully aware or cognizant at the time that such a change has taken place, and it may even take him several years to fully appreciate the nature of the change which has occurred in his mind and in his body.

These experiences, in themselves, can all be lumped roughly or grouped together in what might be called the psychic transition; it is most important as you, yourself, have told people — the first psychic transition is the one that will lead them upward from the low path of reactionary thinking into a more realistic spiritual integration with the higher concepts of life. So, do not despair even though these people with whom you come in contact are most reactionary in nature, and they may or may not accept; they may spurn or they may even seem to turn away from the most beautiful concepts. Yet, remember, it is always in their time and place and in the proper relationships that they must accept these things or these persons will certainly recur and recur again in the realm of experience on the so-called earth or on some similar planet until they learn these integrating factors or concepts. It is a must with everyone, because the innermost nature of every person which links that individual with the higher Self will not cease its continual yearning, its continual infusion into the lower nature of man until it has made itself manifest.

You, yourselves, as expressionists and channels of these Divine Concepts must surely be lifted up, and the burden of karma shall be taken from your shoulders, because these concepts would, if they were not properly expressed into your world at the present time, leave this burden of karma weighing heavily upon your shoulders so that you, too, would want to again reincarnate into this material world of experience until it (karma) was most properly satisfied. Thus, we speak not only for yourselves as personal individuals at this time and place, but we might speak this word of encouragement and understanding to the future persons who thus come in contact with the exact portrayal of life in their sequences about you.

The Master Jesus, as did many Avatars who appeared on the planet earth, also suffered these same burdens and these same recriminations to selfhood; they often asked themselves inwardly, "What was the use of trying to teach such elemental people the higher Principles of the inner natures of themselves?" It was always in the trying and in the questing of the Inner Self that they rose above these thoughts, and the answer would always come clearly and plainly to them from the Higher Selfhood which was within the Mastership of Soul Self so that they must always rise above these conditions, this being the determining element, the strength of character, the unity and purpose of the Divine Selfhood in its expression and in its relation to the Infinite.

I may roughly sum up our visit here on this plateau.

We shall not attempt, at this time, to enter into the many various temples and buildings, the different centers of dwellings which we may call dormitories, for want of a better name; these elements would all be tremendously interesting and very vital to your understanding. They all relate as very functional orders of integration in the lives and in the manner of conduct in daily — pardon the term 'daily' — living, because the sun does not rise and set on this planet. Life here is a continual infusion of the most Divine, permeating energies of God's High Nature. We live not from moment to moment but with a complete realization of the infusion of this energy within everything, not only within us, but it is pulsating and radiating externally in everything that we do and see. How different indeed, with the selfhood and in the false external ego structures of the individual on the earth plane. He has, as you have so aptly termed it, 'dug himself a little pit of clay' wherein he wallows in this mire of selfhood 'til he can peer over the edge and see something beyond the immediate horizons of the clay bank in which he is so firmly mired in his materialisms.

In exploring these numerous buildings and going into the teaching Centers here, you would again find students who are to reappear in various astral and terrestrial worlds in the future; students who are studying the most extended concepts of the psychokinetics or the extension of the mind forces. This learning will enable the individual to infuse the desire and the ability within himself to learn or to become integrated with the wisdom and knowledge which is stemming through the spiritual consciousness of the teacher, as he is reaching through the minds and inner consciousness of these people. These mentions are not necessarily merely words which are spoken in the native tongue or portrayed in such picturization of books or texts as might be available to students or teacher, but the most high essences of these teachings will be permeations and radiations from the

Higher Self, which will lock and interlock each individual, each group of students with their teacher so that they, too, become infused with the higher natures and the higher values of the spiritual self of the teacher. I do hope I have made my point clear on this particular subject, because it is of the most vital importance for everyone to understand. The most valuable, the most beautiful, and the most virtuous of all things which come into the expression of every living being do not come from the veil of experience, but become integrations of the Higher Self and from the infusions of the Higher Self as the individual learns through experience to separate himself from this experience and to seek the higher state of selfhood which is linked with the most infinite nature of Infinity. He shall find the ultimate answers, the ultimate destiny, and the ultimate realizations of all things in which Infinity is. So, until such future time, my dear ones, when we meet again — our love to you all.

— St. Teresa.

(Ruth asked a question regarding the former St. Teresa, as to whether she was the one whom Jesus raised from the dead — Lazarus' daughter.) Reply — "That is correct, dear. I also served a reincarnation in Europe during the Reformation."

CHAPTER XCVIII

Good day, friends. I am a former printer of Philadelphia and had the great honor of being one of the signers of the 'Declaration of Independence' and was probably better known as "Poor Richard". There is a widely publicized version of my life in discovering electricity by flying a kite. I welcome this opportunity of returning — at least in a vocal way — to my beloved country of America to re-establish a more personal contact with the lives, not only of the citizens, but with the leaders of the various governmental orders as they now exist in our great country. Even though it has been some years and I have almost forgotten how long, (170 years), but many years have passed since I lived among you, yet my heart is still loyal and filled with many fond memories and recollections of my life there in the early days of America. I have been quite active in keeping some sort of mental contact with the heads of the government during the many years and have watched very closely the progress of America. I would like to say, also, that I have bec ' part of an organization of former leaders of America such as George Washington and Abraham Lincoln, and many others of the original Signers of the Declaration of Independence. We have been working, whenever an opportunity presented itself, to inspire or to lead in whatever small way that we felt would best serve the general welfare of the American people, in their destiny and in their future evolutions as the leader and the greatest nation of the world.

You must all know that it has been truly set up and conceived by the Divine Minds and Intellects of the higher Celestial Kingdoms, and with the interpretations of this great God Intelligence, that America has been destined to fulfill, to the largest measures, the prophecies of the Bible in connection with the building of the "New Jerusalem". Through the future leadership and expres-

1093

sion of such leadership in the years to come, America will truly bear the fruit of the tree which will be eaten by the nations of the world. This is the fruit of peace.

I am normally associated here in the third plane of the great city of Unarius and integrate my activities most conducively with those of the third Center of the whole structure of Unarius as it was known to you as the Center of Philosophy. It is in this connection, of course, as you study the histories that I wrote a great deal in Philadelphia along these philosophical lines, and there were many mottoes which were left behind and have been of some use to various people who have picked them up.

Now, getting back to the subject of the present and future of America, I shall devote most of this time to speaking about the present and future rather than to explore or take you directly in contact with any of the buildings which are immediately before you. We will just pause quietly and talk about a few things which are developing upon the present horizon of the conditions of the world; and while these things are of the utmost importance, at the moment, yet, it will surely be seen that of the morrow they shall pass. At present, there is considerable pressure being brought about by the great nation overseas to dissolve what is called the Nato or the Organization of Allied Nations, which has been set up as a defensive measure to curb the spread of communism. However, this great Dragon from the East which is sometimes wrongly called the 'Bear' is writhing most forcibly and in the most subtle ways to try to free herself from the coils of restriction which have been set about her by the Western peoples.

It should be very apparent to the leaders of the nations that these are only subterfuges, and while pressures may be brought to bear on one front, they are secretly entering the back door of some other nations for the purposes of conquest. We could warn the leaders of America today that Russia is planning a 'coup de grace' by capturing India; that is her next step and is quite possible within the next year and a half, as Russia has — in the plan as it was set down many years ago — given the year 1958 as the ultimate for the attainment of India. We can give you other dates from time to time as to when Russia will enter into some new dominion of conquest. As a whole, I believe that the leaders of America are quite well acquainted with this psychological trick, that it is the purpose of this great nation to instigate riots and various other destructions of the world while she secretly prepares some great stroke of conquest.

Now, I know that the purpose of this book is to spread Truth and to acquaint the average individual with the higher purposes of the Spiritual Leadership, yet, all in all, we must always start at the bottom of the ladder before we can climb to the top. It resolves itself, therefore, into such progressive steps as relate themselves to the different integrated factors of your daily life and in the pursuance of life, liberty, and happiness much as it is in your present day with all of the modern conveniences and methods of transportation and communication. You are not isolated nor are you immune to the policies of your neighbors across the sea, and this is a very well-known and much regrettable fact. Of the future years of America which lie ahead, we can say that the next three or four years will be, perhaps, just as critical as in any time through which America has ever passed. We would say that it was much more critical than when the British burned Washington in 1812. We would also warn the people of America that her danger, if war should happen, will not be from the air. Russia has under construction and has had for a long time, a fleet of atomically powered submarines which are remotely controlled and which will travel not only through the water, but also on the bottom of the ocean, and will climb the beaches of your shores and explode these atomic missiles in your very back yards. Russia is building bombers, but this is only a front to create the impression that she is air-minded.

Russia gave up the idea of bombing America many years ago in view of the strong defensive measures which were taken after the close of World War II. The leaders of America would be wisest to bend every effort scientifically and otherwise to create defensive measures along the ocean floors at least three or four miles from the various beaches of the country.

The harbors, too, will not be immune from these submarine monsters which creep along the bottom of the ocean on caterpillar treads or can be projected through the water with incredible speed. There will be many other problems which will confront America in the future which relate to a more personal nature than these dangers overseas. Do not feel too frightened by this great Dragon as we call this nation across the sea, in the immediate present, for as long as this Dragon is pacified with the tempting morsels of other nations which she can gobble up she will not turn her attention to your shores. However, sooner or later, the most tender of these morsels will be devoured and she will look across the seas to America. As a very wily and wise Beast which has been described in the book of Revelations, (Bible), this great Power will continually try to form such conquests without the price of human blood or the struggle of war, which is not only very expensive but is also very dangerous for both sides in this atomic age. I am most unhappy to bring you this very distracting news and did so much against the judgment of some of my other compatriots here in these great Centers; however, I have been once, and will be always, a great lover of America and I still consider myself a loyal citizen to the cause of Democracy; though these warnings may not fill a page in your book, or if they do, they will not be the prettiest things to read, yet, they may be very vital warnings to the leaders of the nations in the future.

The Center here which you are presently visiting, as I mentioned, is connected and integrated with the philosophical plane of Aurelius, and here it is that we may give you a little something more optimistic in nature; for along with the other Centers, considerable and hasty preparation — if we can be accused of being hasty — has been made in preparing some of the future generations of leaders and peoples who will migrate, through reincarnation, to the planet earth to become leaders of different factions of human relationship. I can promise you, and you may rest assured, that there will be leadership of such brilliance and intensity as has never before been demonstrated upon the face of the planet earth. It shall surpass anything which you can now envision in your mind. To say that America and the nations of the world will exist in a unified brotherhood in the future hundreds of years is not only a definite possibility but is a fact, and one which will arrive and conclude after the slaying of the great Dragon which is the last of the four great Beasts.

Such brotherhood, too, shall tear down all the constrictive centers of racial hatred and prejudices as they now exist among the earth people; it shall, also, tear down much of the factionalism of the present religious systems or various theosophical orders as they are now in existence on the earth. Such great spiritual leadership shall come forth which will unite the people so that even the political leadership shall pass from existence, and such governments as will exist in those future days will be primarily vested with high spiritual authority and great benevolence and love for humanity. They will also be coupled with the higher realms of these Centers of Shamballa; I should say, Unarius. I, too, am having some difficulty with the new name, but it is a fine name so we will persist. The point I was making was that there will be a return to that ancient and time-honored system in which God really and truly does rule man; and that God does not, in a sense, rule, but becomes an integrated part of the individual as well as of the collective masses of the people; and in such unified brotherhood, there will come the greatest peace and blessings which have ever been known to the races of mankind. Yes, there will be a flag waving over that great 'City of Jerusalem' in the future, and this great flag will be composed largely of the many states of the great Nation of America. May you always find peace in Infinite Consciousness.

— Benjamin Franklin.

CHAPTER XCIX

Yes, what has been spoken is true. It is in the future of the planet earth and in the many races of people who are now coming and going, that these people, in themselves, will properly, through the law of reincarnation and frequency vibration, come and go upon the many other terrestrial and spiritual planets so that they too, shall find a future time and a future day in that great world to come. The very elements of the planet, itself, will have changed and become much more spiritual in nature; the fruits of Heaven shall grow and be borne upon the trees of the earth, and the minds of the people shall be filled with love so that their hearts, too, shall beat in unison.

This plane or plateau of Unarius is the third from the base of the great city, as was explained to you, and while I am not normally associated with this Center of Unarius, it was most favorable that I visit at this time to converse on some rather weighty matters which were confronting the immediate destiny of America. As Benjamin pointed out to you, the next few years will be very critical ones, indeed, for America. There are at present great stresses and tensions being expressed in the underlying structures in the great nations; and from these present day events the foundation is being laid for some very important future transpositions. Oh, I am having much difficulty here with the words; it will be a happy day when all people do not speak with a flopping piece of flesh in their mouths, but can converse truly within themselves with each other. Words are sad things and can be distorted and twisted around so that nothing comes out of the heart.

However, let us continue. I would be most happy at this time to show you if you wish to go into some of the buildings; while it is much the same here as you might see in many of the other Sections, yet there are some very great philosophers and other literary minds as well as some musical talent who are gathered in the great Center of Unarius. They are becoming acquainted and unifying themselves so that in a few years or perhaps a hundred years or so, many of them will appear upon your earth. If I may put in a little personal observation, the earth could use some new talent in many different fields at the present time. Music is, in your present day, suffering from malnutrition.

Art also, has become something which defies description and there are very few people who are sufficiently well versed with the brush or the pen on your earth today who could even be considered students of some of the Masters of the past. Now, I do not wish anyone to take offense at this. It is far from my desire to arouse any antagonism in the breasts of any individuals, but let these things lie where they may, because they are purely factors which are relevant to the time and the place or the age in which some nation or some planet is at the present time revolving.

Not too many years in the future, the people of the earth will be acquainted with people from other planets through space travel. It will not come from developments by your own science, but it will come because these people land and make actual contact with the government leaders. The past years have been of such nature that people have been gradually prepared for this great event; many people are being conditioned by the repeated observations of these flying objects, so that, in the future years they will not be alarmed when the actual contact will be made. Through these contacts there will be a great deal more of the constructive and elevating sciences which will be brought to the people of the earth from some of these more highly developed planets, not only outside of the solar systems, but from some of the other places which are even beyond the universe as you know it today.

Yes, it may even be possible for the planet Lemuria

to re-establish a new contact with the earth, just as it was done more than 150,000 years ago. These things will, all in themselves, be brought about in the future years, even before you both, shall I say, "kick the frame"! Yes, you are seeing right, for we have presented to you and we can describe to you the man you are seeing. He comes from one of these distant planets in a far off solar system; he is a very tall, slender man, dressed in a simple one-piece suit that looks like a tight fitting pair of red tights; he dresses from the top of his head to the tip of his toes in this red suit which is made of a very sparkling, synthetic bright red material similar to spun glass. These people on this planet all dress this way. Now, you will see many strange sights in the future. As you have been told, Parhelion will soon make a very close conjunction with the earth within the next few years. You must refer back to the opening chapters of your book to find the right date, but it shall arrive some time before 1975. During this time there will be many wonderful things happen about the earth, not only in the political fields — and that almost makes me shudder just to think of the word 'political' — but in the scientific world as well.

There will also come some new spiritual leaders, from out of the masses and multitudes of the people, with the new science of the future, just as you, yourself, are trying to teach some of the people about you. These leaders will give great strength to the philosophy of life as you are now teaching to people. From here and there all around you there will come much more of these things about which you are hearing. It will indeed be a great and wonderful age which is being ushered in to the people of the world and there is an end in sight for many of the grievous ills of the past years. The fear of war and the fear of many unseen and unheard of things which give rise to new fears shall be banished from the hearts and minds of the people with the new Light of Spiritual Science which shall come into their lives. Pardon the delay, I was just waiting for something to pass; (R.R. train), but I do believe it will serve our purpose for the moment if we shall discontinue as I see now that the power is beginning to become a little dim. So, take courage for the future; do not become personally or emotionally involved in the various idiosyncracies of the people with whom you come in contact. To thoroughly and fundamentally understand the basic underlying psychological motivations of these people will give you great strength and courage; it will give you great philosophy to overcome and to circumvent their numerous projections of ego; they, in themselves, just as little children, must touch the candle flame of life before they can become acquainted with its values so they may not harm or hurt you. Just feel secure that you are fulfilling your own destiny and your own mission, as you so did set this great plan in motion and become part of this plan. It is in the deliverance of this plan that you are progressing further along in the evolution of your life, and you will very quickly reach the place where you need not return to the lower dimensions to work out these purposes.

However, these concepts will be explained to you and I believe that you will become consciously aware of them more and more, as the developments of the future. So now let us rest in Peace.

— Meng Tse.

CHAPTER C

Four score and seven years ago, our fathers conceived a new nation. Greetings, loved ones. I have come for this occasion from a distant neighboring planet of Clarion, one that is more properly known to the earth and to some of the people as Vulcan. Vulcan, as you have been given the information, is the planet of a spiritual nature which is of a somewhat higher rate of vibration — using the language of the scientist — wherein the colored man makes a certain spiritual evolution. In leaving the planet earth, if the colored person — and if I can pause for a moment to explain this cycle situation — who has a dark skin may have advanced spiritually to a point where he feels there are certain elements, certain factors of progression or integration, or he may have felt in some way the quickening of the spirit, so he will wish to further this evolution of his soul consciousness, then he shall come to the planet Vulcan. It is in this dimension and on this planet he will find such suitable companionship and environment which will be most helpful for his future development. I would say, too, the colored man is primarily — as far as the basic and elementary tribes of jungle people who have existed on the earth and who have been oppressed into slavery are concerned — a creature of a comparatively primitive state of development. While there is a certain line of demarcation where we might say there is the infusion of the God force, or the God Intelligence into every human, yet, it must be remembered this God Force does not come in one lifetime or in one generation. This life force must be the gradual development of consciousness within the individual through his numerous evolutions. We say that the colored man, primarily, as you know him in the early stages of his development on the planet earth, as he was first found in the jungles, was a creature who had evolved through

1103

certain integrations of evolutions from some of the lower structures.

As man comes into the domain or the dimension in which the newly born human could actually be called man, this point in his evolution was the place in which the actual contact of the superconsciousness entered into his development; so he begins his climb through the various terrestrial and astral spheres and dimensions. Always with each succeeding regeneration and rebirth he becomes quickened so that there is much more of that contact with the Higher Self.

The planet Vulcan, itself, serves — in the capacity for the black man as far as his environment is concerned in this state of his development — just as the planet Venus serves for the white man. He is not immune to the planet earth; there are many other terrestrial planets where the man who has a darkened skin may reside although he does not always, by necessity, have to have a dark skin. You might be interested to know that on one planet there are actually albino black men; that is to say, these people all maintain the same racial characteristics; they are in the same comparative stage of spiritual development or evolution. The prime purpose of conveying to you some of the descriptions of these people is one which has a two-fold meaning; one which is, of course, the most important, is the fact that we are conveying to you the idea of spiritual development through the races of mankind. In such development, man must become aware that whatever the color or texture of his skin or body may be does in no way set him apart and make him different in the sight of God. He is still that same man who is developing and evolving through the countless dimensions which will enable him to make a closer contact with that God-Self, or Higher Self.

On the planet Vulcan we find certain picturizations of environment quite similar in some respects to the various astral worlds which you have visited. There you will find the same radiant structures as you found on the planet Venus. The differences here will be, of course, the manner in which these various buildings, cities, and dwelling places are so constructed, as they will be more suitable to the way in which the black man has found his development on some terrestrial planet. Yes, you might find even the thatched huts, just as they were in the jungles; the differences here are in the fact that the black man has built these thatched huts from the radiant energies with which he is surrounded because even the very nature of the plants, the grasses, and the trees with which he is surrounded is of that same radiant energy nature. While he may gather the grasses of the field or the swamp to thatch this hut, yet, they are not the grasses of the field or the swamp which he might gather in the jungle. So with this difference before him at all times, he becomes gradually quickened of the spirit. You will find other stages of development on this planet Vulcan which are quite similar in these respects of divisional dimensions, just as you would find on Venus.

In the higher dimensions you will find the colored man functioning much the same as he would function on your planet earth. You will find him associated in laboratories, in hospitals, in clinics, in libraries, and in other highly developed Centers of learning just as he would on the planet earth or even much more so.

There are certain cities or places of development on the planet Vulcan which are very much more advanced than those on the earth; it is in such environment that the colored man will be enabled, in the future, to develop to a point in his mentality where he can appear in a terrestrial dimension such as the earth. He will no longer have the colored skin because he has developed to a point where he has removed much coloration from his skin. The fanciful story of Cain and Abel, as portrayed in the Old Testament of the Bible, is a sad dereliction of truth which originally was conveyed in a parabolistic form, but has lost even the semblance to its own original portrayal or meaning. The problem of skin coloration, or shall I say subcutaneous pigmentation as it has been called by the scientist in the terrestrial dimension, is a protective layer against the highly actinic rays of the sun. This would however, be very necessary on the planet Vulcan if the colored man were in physical form. Man does not live on the planet Vulcan in the physical form.

Now, I can hear people firing all kinds of questions when they read these lines. What makes a man colored, and what is the purpose of this particular state of evolution, or is it necessary for everyone to become colored at some one time, and numerous other questions. These inquiries can all be answered by remembering the individual concept, and as he so conceived in his own mind through the lower orders into the higher orders, that the basic idea of skin coloration is one which was developed primarily through the processes of protection. It is also quite obvious that a person who wishes to enter into the terrestrial world through the doorway of the womb is not always of such a spiritual nature that he is able to determine who or what his parents are. Many people who enter the doorway or into this lower order of their evolution find themselves as colored. Others, too, may purposely evolve into this race for the purpose of leadership or to such other benefits as their own mentality or spiritual growth may have entitled them to this form of leadership.

These problems, in themselves, are all very divers and are subject to innumerable interpretations. No one is impelled to take on the evolution wherein he becomes a person who has a colored skin. It must be remembered, that in the abstract consciousness, as a person resides in the spiritual dimension, these concepts do not take on the proportions which they are given in the terrestrial dimensions. They do not assume the same consequence. They do not have the same importance, nor do they appear to be even a factor or a 'principle of any importance in many cases.

However, I must not dwell too lengthily upon this topic as it is certainly one which is rather touchy in nature, not only to the white man but to the colored person as well, and one in which every individual must, through his own proper reasoning faculties, find some sort of an answer. It would require many hours of discussion to fully reveal to you all of the facts and ramifications which are pertinent to these interpretations.

I would dwell a few moments, if I may, upon the future racial integration, as it will exist in the coming America. As you have watched the colored man in his own environment in the cities and in the countries about you, you have noticed that there has been a tremendous amount of inter-marriage between both whites and the colored as well as other yellow races from across the Pacific Ocean. America can be considered to be something like a huge melting pot of humanity wherein these various and numerous races of the world are being inter-mixed as we would mix some huge batter for a cake. Many people are too much concerned with this problem. They have not the proper perspective of spiritual values which are contained in the evolution of man. They should be more primarily concerned with the levels of mentality and to the amount of integration which can be achieved by breaking down the various barriers which exist between the different races. The great racial differences stem, not primarily from skin coloration, but from evolutionary principles of which man is unaware.

In the future of America the people will achieve much of that unity and harmony between the various races of people; even much more than has already been achieved.

Going completely into the future years, you will find mankind not so much concerned with the color of his skin, but more interested in the capacity of his service to humanity and to the mental level from which he exists. He will also be judged according to the spiritual values of his nature. The older orders of racial hatreds and separations will no longer exist. I would say also, in conclusion, that although my life was rather violently terminated by an assassin, and also that I have been criticized many times for what are considered some mistakes in policies, yet, always these deeds were done with the utmost thought and consideration. These things were also done with what I believed was from Divine guidance. So, it will be in the future with others. I will most humbly serve, not only my country but all the purposes, all the fulfillments and all the attainments which will be possible for man to achieve; and I will serve him as best I can to attain and to achieve all of these things. May God bless you and America!

— Abe Lincoln.

CHAPTER CI

I guess I will take command then. I have the identity of Wolfgang Mozart and it has been said that at one time there was a celebration of the birthday of my coming into the earth plane, and there was some talk about the various things which were done in the line of musical compositions at my very early age of childhood. However, your history books will tell you of these things and I need not dwell on them too lengthily. Yes, you are very right — there are many here with you this evening at this time — as you are connected directly to the Fourth Plane of the great Center of Unarius which links it back directly again to the fourth planet of Muse and Coralanthus. As you remember, this was the planet where all of the musicians, poets, literary minds, and the various associated artists gathered during the working out of some of their spiritual cycles so they may return to some earth habitation at some future day which would enable them to give much more of these wonderful arts with which we are surrounded.

Like Coralanthus, this plane too, is devoted to instruction in leadership in the various arts as they were explained to you from Coralanthus. You may not notice a slight oriental accent which I have as Djwal Kul is here with me and assisting in this transmission. Sometimes these inflections do get in, even though we may have been widely separated by periods of time. He is working very close to your present situation, and is frequently making contacts with Ruth through the incense; he smiles when I mention this, and shows me a small box he carries in his pocket. (They are merely joking, as they emit the effulgences from their very being.)

Now, you are looking around you and see that like the beautiful planet of Muse, here too, it carries its own distinct, though very subtle colorations, just as was so evident upon that planet. Going into these different Centers where the classrooms are conducted, there will be much more of the highly advanced sciences of the different interpretive arts as they have been expressed in drama, or literature, or in such kindred and associated arts in the different planetary systems. The main idea here, too, as in the other Centers of Unarius, is to acquire some specific type of leadership. The one big thing which is active in my mind at the present time of which you are no doubt quite aware is that on your earth today music is in rather a sad state of neglect. This you need not despair, because it merely means that you are going through a change or a cycle and in such a condition it is like the time when you take a bath and you are partly naked and partly clothed; so it is with the changes. There is really nothing outside which bears a semblance to the form or to what it will be when the cycle is fully completed or, as the man is clothed. In the future years, we here intend to do something about that sad state of affairs, and there will come into the planet earth a great renaissance of music which will be beyond even those wonderful days of which I was so fortunate to be a part, back in the period of the Reformation! The music I might mention, incidentally, will be composed largely of instrumentation and of such chord structures and chromatics which will have a considerable amount of the healing virtues or essences which will be quite necessary to suit the mental temperament or the spiritual advancements and needs of the people of the earth at that time.

I see you are noticing a very large and beautiful temple which is immediately before you, with a huge dome which seems to be fluted upon the top. It might be worthy to note that the front of this large building also looks something like the mansion in which Thomas

Jefferson lived, called Monticello, which has large supporting columns in the front portico. This huge dome is especially constructed so that these various sections look something like the segments of an orange. Each one is constructed of a different type of crystal energy so that it transmits its own particular band of frequency structures from the Radiant Energies as they are stemming in from the outside vortexes of space.

Going into this temple, you see that this is rather a large circular space which has many fluted columns rising around on the outside diameter. There are no seats in this center space, but rather a very large beautiful fountain of Radiant Energy. The various teachers or students are wont to stroll around this fountain and converse during the periods of their classes and as they pass through the various rays of light or energy which are projected from this beautiful dome, are thus inspired and strengthened and renewed in much the way you would feel had you eaten a very wonderful meal; only the difference here would be that it would be much more spiritual in nature, so these students and teachers are much refreshed to go back into their classrooms. Branching out from this temple are five different very large wings which unite and serve in their various orders of function; just as you saw the temple in Coralanthus, these too, serve in the different parts of the interpretive arts.

I have been checking over the different instrumentations and instruments which we combine together in the symphony orchestra, and I have also been checking up on such sundry modifications or improvements. It is well to note that music, like all other things, has its evolution and its time; however, it is one of the peculiarities of the earth people to cling to the things of the past rather than to remake or to further take full advantage of the evolution of time as they are progressing through that period. So it is with the musical instruments; they are very wonderful and very serviceable for the types of music which they are at the present portraying. They were largely and basically modifications of some existing structures of horns which were used by the more primitive peoples, or the reeds of flutes were such as were derived from the type which the shepherds used on the hills; or we might go into the jungles and see our kettle drums being used by the savages as they stretched a skin upon a hollow log. So, these things have really come down to man through the ages as mere modifications and they were slowly changed by the condition of time that really, man has not actually invented a new musical instrument for 'heaven only knows' how long.

However, the future will hold many new inventions of musical instruments which will bear no resemblance to any which you now use. They will be largely such instruments which will be electronic in nature or they will use crystals and various other types of materials which are now not generally known to the earth scientist or to the earth musician. I might point out that many of the new types of molecular crystals which you call the various germanium or such other substances, will be found on the earth either synthetically or through other means; man will learn to put these numerous types of crystals to new uses; and coupled together with the science of electronics, great strides will be made in the dimension of music. Color, too will play a large part in the future symphony orchestra; color will not only be visible but there will be many invisible colors which will also be used with the symphony orchestra.

The very loud percussive instruments will largely pass in the future, as man will be much more sensitive in his nature and will not be able to endure these heavy percussive sounds. Man will also develop new trends or tendencies away from the old periods of tragedy as they were expressed in the operas of the past, or to such heavy vibratory tone structures which depicted the wrath of the elements or such other of the more elemental forms of music.

Thus, music will develop into a much more spiritual tenure and will be largely suggestive of the music of the spheres or of the Celestial dimensions as it is sometimes termed in your language. This will suit the spiritual nature of man in the future.

Stretching out away from this temple which you see in front of you, are numerous other public buildings and dormitories or private dwellings which are used by the teachers and students who are living here at this time. In fact, the whole plane or level of this city is much the same as the other previous ones which you have explored in the lower levels. It is circular in nature and contains other temples and other buildings which are quite functional in their own particular nature. There are other large civic auditoriums and such places where various plays and dances and other expressions are portrayed. However, the main objective for anyone who stays here for any length of time is to obtain a directive force for whatever he has learned in any of the other dimensions of Unarius. I do hope this part of your exploration has served to be satisfactory to you.

I might point out at this time, also, there will come a new science to the world of the future which will be called "The Science of Vibronics". The scientist will learn that through vibration he can pollinate the fruit and flower blossoms of his planet and that he will be able to raise vegetables and fruits in much greater abundance and in a much more prolific nature with the use of vibration. Vibration will become the keynote to the future age, whether it is in music or whether it is in any other form of energy with which man is surrounded, and in which he is actively participating in his daily life. The science of vibronics will largely replace and supplant any of the more ordinary and inefficient methods of energy usage as you know them today. You may even see, in some future reincarnation, automobiles or cars, as you call them now, which will be powered by motors which use energy in the form of vibration from the Cosmic or Celestial dimensions.

This energy is free and is so abundant to use and remains only for the earth scientist to learn how to reach out with the proper implementation to tap this inexhaustible source of cosmic energy. This all resides in the dimension of supersonic frequencies about which the scientist knows nothing today. What he calls supersonic in his own terminology is like the proverbial tortoise against the hare. The future scientist will also learn to use such methods of communication as already have been developed on other planets; or he may even be able to change his body through certain electronic instruments whereby it can be projected upon a beam and arrive at another destination in the split part of a second, to be reassembled instantaneously. These things are actually in existence and in working order in other places and in astral worlds on several of the planets about which I know. The future scientist will be one who is vastly advanced in his knowledge; however, this is not a scientific discussion by any means. I am merely trying to acquaint you with the realm of vibrations because this, in itself, is closely akin to the music world.

A musician such as I was upon the earth, or a composer, if you would call me such, is much like a small infant who is just beginning to walk, in comparison to what he learns about vibration as he goes through the different evolutions and starts his progression by entering Unarius. There is no limit in this field, as in any other field that we contact, because God is vibration or He is Energy, whatever term you wish to call Him; He is everything. So, in the future, you will persist in your effort, and I personally will see that there are certain forces or certain contacts which you will make at suitable times when there are such opportunities for such usages, whereby you, too, can use color harmony and vibration in your future therapies for the various students who come to you.

Music, in the future, will indeed be vastly different from that of your present day. I am very interested in your Hi-Fi system, as you call it — that you have built — and the music is very realistic as compared to the actual reproduction of the symphony orchestra. The records, incidentally, which Ruth has been buying occasionally were not bought just because she was attracted in any way to them; it was actually suggested that she buy them simply for the reason that these three particular records were, especially, quite productive of some rather unusual tone and harmony combinations; in the future, if she studies them much more closely, she will learn something more of vibration, of color, and harmony.

However, I do not wish to overstay my leave. There are other great composers here, at least they were listed as 'great composers' in their earth time — such as Beethoven and Franz Liszt. I could name several others with whom you are quite familiar serving as teachers and students here in this plane. Several other figures who were quite notable in singing roles in the operas such as Enrico Caruso are on this plane and are at the present time taking some study courses in some unusual vibronics which they will use in a future day. And so, dear ones, may we meet again soon.

— Wolfgang.

CHAPTER CII

A loaf of bread, a jug of wine and thou. Omar Khayyam.

I would just take this opportunity for only one brief statement, if I may; Kahlil Gibran is here with me, and we wish you to know we are very close to you and working with you for the future evolution and to bring into your world the beauties of man's most innate nature. We will, from time to time, bring to you such poetry or such writings and literature which may be considered acceptable in an inspirational way, and which will also factually portray to man, in this inspiration, that which will lift him and give him courage. It will also give him an answer to many of the problems with which he is struggling. These writings and works will, in themselves, be very catalytic in nature; to read them will give the proper intonations, the various chord structures, which will contain all of the elements of spiritual therapy which you call inspiration. We were with you through the past year and helped you to compose the various things which you have in your writings at the present time; and we shall continue to be with you whenever you feel that we can best serve you. Sit quietly in such moments of inspiration and we shall come to you. We are with Elisha, Ezra, and Enoch and many of the others who are working as your God-parents and your guides and your inspirers in your work upon the earth. Always know that we are with you. This is just a small personal message, and need not be included in your large book if you do not desire to place it there, as my friends are giving a very factual description as they take you from place to place.

However, I am very closely connected to this plane as a former poet and writer upon the earth, just as many of my colleagues here are, so, quite naturally, you would find me working here from time to time among the students. It has been a long time since I was upon the earth, at least so it seems to me now, and I have no wish to return. However, there are still some memories which occasionally come to me from the akashic records, or I may pick up some book or piece of literature which connects me with the past with some of the numerous scenes of my life upon the earth. People, too, come and go from that period of time and we renew acquaintances or exchange stories of such familiar anecdotes as happened to us in the past.

There is a king, or at least if he will pardon me calling him a king, who is called Nebuchadnezzar who is standing quite close to me at this time. Nebuchadnezzar, as you know, was a king of Babylonia and he had a very personal contact with you at one period of time. However, if such opportunity exists in some of the future writings, he will come to you, too, to assist in these various translations. I may close momentarily now.

— Omar.

CHAPTER CIII

This is a most gracious pleasure. You may call me Djwal Kul. I lived in China a long time ago, also in India and in Tibet; so, I had much of the earth philosophy and was able to come back at this time and teach this philosophy. I could have been called a Yogi, but I will not spend too much time on myself; if you are more curious you can look into the books and find something more about these times, although I am considered something of a mysterious figure to many who are in the occultisms.

Now, tonight we shall take a little journey to the fifth plane of integration of Unarius; this is the plane which is linked up and functions directly with Parhelion on the center plane of Eros. As you already know, this is the scientific plane where there are some very wonderful and highly developed scientists who are working in the great forces of the universe. You may, perhaps, think it odd that I would be giving you this message or help conduct you through this Center, or you might have thought some great scientist would come along, but it is not always so. I remember in my earth life we knew about atomic structures, and we taught these principles and concepts pertaining to the structures of matter and the universe to our gurus and to others about us, so who can say that we were not quite scientific? I do pride myself in knowing something of the great cosmic and Celestial universes; so perhaps everything will be all right after all.

The actual fifth plane is one which is quite serviceable in so many respects to the great scientific minds who must come here to learn how to be able to relate themselves in such a way to these struggling masses of humanity that this knowledge will become useful to them in their evolution. Here again, you will find many of the

1118

resemblances to the great city of Parhelion in the general color harmony and in the outlines and the various functions of the buildings; you will find great laboratories here that are used for research work into the more highly developed principles of, shall I call it in the language of your earth scientists, parapsychology, and it is largely from these Centers here in Unarius that we are working with you to conduct your classes, and much of the material you get comes directly from this Center.

As you look about you, you will see, as usual, the same beautiful energy structures made of these refined substances of the radiant energies which are closely bound together with thought forces. When the earth scientist has mastered this principle to some degree, it will indeed open up a whole new world to him. He has, in a synthetic way, composed literally thousands of synthetic substances, but these substances are all, in themselves, very dead and lifeless. He has not yet learned that in order to put molecules and atoms together or to change atoms, one must know something about life, and the thing of which the life or the molecule is. If it does not have its correct linkage or relationship with its mother vortex – and it is something like a baby nursing on the nipple – the atom or the molecule is lifeless. Your synthetic substances are quite serviceable for the things for which they have been invented, yet, this whole synthetic synthesis of molecular structures is quite lifeless and does not possess the true qualities of the organic or the inorganic elements of the earth. While you may call them organic or inorganic and they may be inanimate or without motion, or they may grow, it makes little difference. All atoms in their uninhibitive state, as they stem from the Mind of God contain life.

The scientist has not yet succeeded in isolating this mysterious force in his test tube and which he will never do until he understands what is behind these great principles of the Life Force of God. So, he must continue to search. But enough of my chatter; I will let you look about you here and, if possible, we will take a little peek into one of the buildings and see what is going on, as we know you are quite pressed for both time and energy. We, too, are most anxious to conclude this first volume in view of the other events which are soon to transpire in your earth life. We are most anxious that this should be brought about very quickly so it will serve the best purposes for all concerned. Therefore, do not feel disappointed if these chapters or the little ribbons (on the recorder) are not printed quite long enough. They shall serve quite adequately for what we have to tell you, and we do not wish to bore you.

Now, this big building which you see before you is a huge structure that could easily put most of your earth buildings to shame, if I can be so crude or informal as to point out such deficiencies. However, it is indeed a very large structure, as you see, and within its boundaries, or its walls — if we can call those pure vibrating energies which are glittering and glowing before you as walls of a building — are literally thousands of minds which are busily engaged in various highly developed and scientific processes, the like of which would mean little or nothing to the earth mind and would not even mean too much to the scientist. So we will just group men together with a more or less small description to say that in this building are primarily grouped the individuals who will in a future day, to a large extent, reincarnate or appear in the terrestrial planet earth. They will, in their due course of time, be those who will carry much of the knowledge in their psychic bodies; and in their relationship and in their maintenance of their vibration here with this Center, they will be able to bring into your world a host and a multitude of new and wonderful inventions. But these things you will see, will not be brought about until man learns to use his mind and to use the energies

1120

more directively. As he exists on the planet earth today it would merely mean that if you gave him more time, he would only spend it dangling his heels over some bar, or he might be in some other difficulty or trouble; so, in the future he must learn to use his time in a more productive way or state of consciousness, otherwise, he would quite naturally become worse than a useless parasite or a toadstool growing upon a tree-stump, and this is quite against his own true spiritual nature.

Deeply rooted within the heart and mind of every individual is that desire to come closer and closer to the great Infinite Godself; that is what makes so many people curious about things which are called occult, or elements of spiritual phenomena or things of that nature. Here in this building, you will see people who are going about in various ways and setting up organizations which will enable them to contact many other individuals who will find themselves together again in these future hundreds of years in the history of the earth; these people will all come together in a more or less unified situation whereby they can lead man into further sunshine and light. Pausing on the threshold of this huge building, which is dedicated to the future sciences of the earth, to peer inside and look about the various buildings would be a revelation in itself; and, as in many of these so-called 'classrooms' or such Centers, they are about the size of some large city, or they may contain such vastness of distances of space; and in their different confines you will find many laboratories, many of the smaller partitions, or the separations which you may call dimensions, or which can be called other things, for the sake of avoiding confusion to separate these things into a more useful relationship one to another so that one can quickly find what he is seeking.

We find many of the various Adepts or Initiates who come here from other Centers, and even though they may be the future poets, writers, or various other of the interpretive arts, they may also be just about anything that you care to choose to name; yet, they come here because they like to learn something more of the way in which this wisdom they have learned can be more adequately expressed in a lower terrestrial dimension. And although science may never be related to them in these lives, yet back somewhere in the reaches of the psychic self there is the wisdom and the knowledge which they have incurred here. It speaks to their personality, we shall say, and gives them the power of delivery or projection. These concepts and the assuredness of wisdom is a wonderful weapon which can be used against the forces of darkness, and always these forces will flee from this flaming sword. For Truth is the wonderful fumigator which will drive out these blacknesses from these different worlds.

To complete the diameter of this Fifth Center would, like many of the others, occupy you for many, many years; in fact, you may spend several hundred years of your earth time. However, be not concerned here about the word 'time' for it means little or nothing, and as it was so adequately explained, time is only a measure whereby you tick your little earth lives away until you mark the time when you will come closer to this Great God. So, be not concerned with this thing of time.

There are other wonderful buildings here in this section, too, which contain the future inventions of the world, and if I were to show you these inventions and explain them to you, you would consider them most fantastic; and if you would not, then perhaps those who read these lines would. But you can rest assured that just about anything which you could imagine, at this time, could very easily exist in these buildings for indeed, man is in a progressive state of evolution. We are primarily concerned with certain limits or boundaries, we shall say, in which scientific knowledge and wisdom can be given to the earth planet as it follows in a cycle that is quite similar in an abstract way to that of a human. It has begun somewhere from the eye or Mind of God as elements, not from some fiery ball which was spewed from the heart of some great sun which has gone berserk; for these elements, in themselves, were transposed in a regular and orderly fashion from the great vortexes of energy from the central Vortex.

The earth scientist has a rather crude and hazy way as to how these planetary systems and suns were developed, but with the passing of time, here too, eyes shall be opened and scales fall away so that he will see the wonders of his universe; and when he does, he will realize just how puny his intellect is at this particular moment. This will make him very humble, and with this humility will come the greatest desire and longing for more knowledge and wisdom. It shall not be a deflation of the ego, but rather a shock which will tear down the false ego structures of self, and the selfhood which he has erected about himself, and in gaining this wisdom and knowledge, he will be able to progress further along the path of evolution.

One of the little problems confronting your human race at this moment is the problem of over-production of the race of mankind himself, and if your present rate of production continues, the earth will face starvation in the next hundred years or so unless adequate means are taken, not only for birth control, but to curb and curtail the inferior strains and races of mankind. Also man must learn the more productive ways in which food can be grown and to utilize such natural sources and resources of food which are still untapped and in existence on the planet earth. The scientist who has pictured the average human of a hundred years hence as taking his meals in a tablet form, is not too far from the actual fact of what might exist, unless these adequate measures are very shortly put into effect. Food is grown very rapidly in such productive areas as to completely debilitate the

1123

soil in a very short period of time, and there is little or no return of the very vital elements. He may think that he is doing so but he does not. The whole science of the human body is built upon some of the intangibles which he at the present time calls enzymes; these enzymes are related in their own way in very complex and abstract concepts with the great life force which stems into the atoms and into the substances which he calls vitamins, enzymes, hormones, and such things which are found in the rebuilding of the processes of the human body, as well as in the control and functioning of these different organs.

Man too, will find in his future days that his taste for certain foods has diminished and he has developed appetites for foods which are now, more or less, foreign to his nature. He may also find that in the future it will be very productive for him to raise crops of insects for food. He will also find crops of other things which he has, as yet, only remotely concerned himself with or considered. For instance, we have one scientist here in this Center named Steinmetz who, on the earth plane, explained to the scientists that the amount of food value which was consumed in yeast in making bread in the world in twenty-four hours, could feed the nation of Germany. Steinmetz went on to postulate such theories with the scientists that through the growing of various bacteria, it would form a very valuable source of supply of food. These are but a few of the untapped sources of food supplies which are yet unrealized by the peoples of the earth.

In the seas there are literally hundreds of millions of tons of very wonderful foodstuffs floating around – and I do not mean the fishes – but this food is called plankton. The whales of the sea feed upon this tiny microscopic animal and filter him through the whalebones of their teeth, by expelling the water through them. Plankton could, in the future, form a very adequate supply of

1124

the protein elements, along with iodine and various other nutritional minerals which are so abundantly found in the marine life. Also such other forms of algae, which you call seaweed, could form very valuable and highly nutritive adjuncts to the diet of the various nations. The idea of continually replenishing your larder from the soil will become increasingly more difficult with the passing of years. These things must all be very seriously considered by the peoples of the future day and age, if they are to continue to live on their little planet earth. The subject of growing food, itself, from the soil is one which is in need of vast improvement from the earth scientist, and as every one of these savants could tell you, the amount of organic minerals or vitamins which is consumed by the plant is indeed very small and almost microscopic. The chief constituents in any of the plant or animal supplies of food are primarily water, for most of your food supplies are at least 85% water. This fact must be borne in mind; the very nutritive elements which are derived from foodstuffs, in themselves, are merely such structures of amino acids, proteins, and various other nutriments which are found in very comparatively small quantities in these foodstuffs. Much labor and much effort has gone into the production of these foodstuffs which could, very easily, be constructed in the laboratory in a molecular way so that man would not need to fear the plague of starvation. One large plant could synthesize sufficient food from the abundance of energy which is about you in the universe to feed the whole nation if it were so that man would need to go on such a diet of pills or capsules; so, in the future, the dweller on the planet earth may sit down to cakes made from bacteria for his breakfast and he may drink synthetic orange juice that has never seen the light of the sun. He may fry his dinner, eat a plankton steak, and such synthetic fruits; these things are entirely within the realm of possibility and are already in existence in other planets in different solar systems to a large degree and to a large extent.

As you know, at least 40 per cent of the food used on the planet Mars is largely synthetic in nature, and they have supplemented what would otherwise be very lean larders, indeed, with the food which they are able to grow in their subterranean cities, because of such lack of space in these comparatively confined dimensions, although, as you know, these small and very wonderful people, are doing very well by themselves in such cities. (Ruth asked the guide here regarding his own personal past life.) To the little Ruth, I am most reluctant to give you some earth history; but I will say that I served once as an Emperor of China; I also served at a later period in the same country as one of the philosophers, and spent a lifetime in Tibet and was known as the Dalai-Lama. I also spent a period of time very close to Krishna in India and also had some experience in Egypt. I hope this will satisfy you until I can come again; meanwhile, you may look around in the books if you are curious. I shall continue to cast my little incense. With all of my love, and our love to you.

— Djwal Kul.

CHAPTER CIV

My brother and sister, I am most happy to be with you again this evening. I am an individual who is not known in the present histories of the earth, and you alone, perhaps, among the millions who inhabit the planet earth at your present day know of my existence. I am Sharamute and, when I greet you as brother and sister, I mean just that, for we were indeed brothers and sister at another time and another place. It might be that my story here with you tonight would be of such nature that we could start in some distant age of several hundred thousand years ago in a great planet named Lemuria in another universe. But for the sake of the readers of this book, I will confine this discussion and chapter to more recent times which will be more compatible to the reasoning natures of the earth individuals. As you were given intuitively, Ernest, that your name is Sharazar and I am Sharamute (twins), we shall continue on that basis. A little later I shall tell you of sister's name, as she was known in Atlantea. However, before we go to this place which we are to visit tonight, we shall ascend first to the plateau of Azore, which is the sixth in ascendency in the great city of Unarius, where we will spend a few brief moments in discussion of the nature of the function of this plateau. As you have been given a book 'Voice of Venus' — the first volume of 'The Pulse of Creation' series — much has already been disclosed to you because here in this plateau we have a continuance of the science of psychotherapy and such phases of spiritual healing and spiritual integration.

Here, in this beautiful city which you see, you are surrounded with these very beautiful crystal buildings, all tinged somewhat with that very subtle tint of blue which corresponds to the basic rate of vibration from the planet Venus. Here, within the walls of this building we find thousands of souls who are learning many of the higher developed methods of healing in the spiritual way with the lost souls on the earth plane. These services, as they are expressed, are not only for the earth, but for many other terrestrial planets in the universe. You will find many thousands of students here, too, who are studying and learning and will reincarnate into the earth to become the doctors, the nurses, the physiotherapists, and various other kinds of practitioners of the future day, who will minister in their own way to the needs of mankind; and I can assure you that it will be very much more advanced than it is at the present time.

Medical science, not only in the fields of pure medicine, but in the fields of psychiatry, as you call it, is much in darkness and much in need of that illumination which will come from the inward revelations of the true self of man, as you know these principles. So, it shall be in the future day when the doctor and the psychiatrist of that day will deal largely with the spiritual natures of man rather than to try and find the elements of disease in his body. So, if you will pardon the brevity of this discourse in this very wonderful city, we will leave this more or less up to your own memory to fill in the details and so integrate these memories in your own minds that you can form a good and definite idea of the function of the plateau of Azore.

Now, we shall go to another great astral world which is whirling about here in this great cosmic Universe of God. The name of this planet is irrelevant, nor would I call it a name, as it is known by many names to many races of people. It is a planet which is devoted mainly to some of the great civilizations of the ages past, as they have existed in a number of the terrestrial dimensions which are in the solar system or in the Universe of the present knowledge of the astrophysicist, as he knows of it at our time. Here, we shall reconstruct for you something of the city and the civilization which was known as Atlantea and which disappeared from the planet earth in a great cosmic explosion which was caused by cosmic disintegration wrongly used by a left hand faction which tried to usurp the power and the hierarchy of the Temple of Amen Ra.

Now that the swirling mists have disappeared from your eyes, you see stretched before you a huge and wonderful city, and you are rapidly descending into the courtyard in front of a huge Temple, which is of the purest and whitest marble. It is very beautiful in its most simple and flowing lines. There is a great Central Tower which rises to the height of over two thousand feet into the air, and would eclipse any of your present skyscrapers and make them look like tiny twigs stuck into the ground. This huge Temple covers many square miles in area and circumference and looks much like the great Temple of Karnac in Egypt, except that it is constructed of the whitest and purest marble. Within its dimensions are not only the temple proper but many residential areas which house the priests and priestesses of the various orders. There is some integration of community life within these temple walls as most of these priests and priestesses carry on normal, ordinary, everyday lives in their own background and are married and often raise families. These officials of this great temple, not only perform the rituals and are the purveyors of the ecclesiastical understandings of the people of the great city which you are seeing about you, but they are also those who dispense what might be termed law, order and justice; however, there are no political systems in this great city nor in this entire empire.

We are somewhere in the period of about 12,000 B.C. according to your Gregorian calendar, and it is the time of the "Festival of the Peacocks". But before we get into this observance and this ceremony, a little more background of not only myself, but of sister Ruth would

1129

be in order here, to make these things more clear to you. She is the High Priestess, and is known as I-O-Shanna, or the "Priestess of the Peacocks". She is not only your sister, at this time, but she is also my sister; and you are known as the "Keeper of Time" in the Central Dome at the top of the great tower. It is your duty to perform many of the astrophysical concepts with which you have been acquainted for many past ages. I have other duties which are more or less connected and linked with officiating at different observances and ceremonies; but come now, the time is almost ripe. "The Ceremony of the Peacocks" is one of a very holy and sacred observance and came down to us many thousands of years ago from a period of time when it was that the great God, Amen Ra visited our planet and our fair city, and he lived here with us for over four hundred days. It was He who gave us, in the great Central Temple which you will see upon the quartz block, the great Flame of Life which has burned brightly ever since.

It has not yet approached the time or the hour when the left hand faction will blast the planet from the face of the earth, for Atlantea is still at peace and is dwelling with the utmost harmony with the great Celestial Powers. While Amen Ra, the God, was here among us then, He was universally loved by all, and He bestowed many and beautiful beneficent gifts to different people; and so when the time of departure came for Him, and He must return to His own Celestial Dimension, there was one who loved Him more dearly than anyone else; she was the then, Priestess of the great Temple and she so bitterly wept at losing the sight of the glorious Amen Ra that she swooned upon the floor, and when she awakened there was before her as a personal gift from this great Lord, a beautiful white peacock. And thus it was that these beautiful birds came to live in the temple of Atlantea; and down through the thousands of years, every year at the exact time of the departure of Amen

1130

Ra, so did the priestesses hold and observe the Ceremony of the departure for this great God.

Now, we have entered the great Central Temple wherein you will see the huge granite triangle which lies in the central part of this temple; it is thirty cubits each way as a triangle, and it is raised about twelve inches from the floor. In the middle of this great triangle there is a large block of the purest white crystal stone; upon this stone there is a huge flame of purest white light which is intensely brilliant and radiant and it glows to a height which is taller than a man. This eternal flame neither moves or sways, nor does it diminish in its brightness, for it has remained thus for thousands of years. Soon you will hear a symphony of the huge temple gongs as they will announce the beginning of the ceremony; these great sounds swell and cascade through the corridors of this temple. As you see, it is in itself, a magnificent structure. The huge columns tower above you for a height of over one hundred feet to the great central vaulted roof, or dome, which is immediately above you. This great dome has large sections of very pure colored crystal which is somewhat familiar and reminds you of the temples you have seen in some of the Centers of Unarius. You must remember that this planet is something of the vibration or rate of Venus and that it is not strictly terrestrial, therefore, all of these things you see about you are somewhat of the same nature of this Radiant Energy with which you have become so well acquainted.

But hark! Now the great gongs are sounding, and with their crashing sounds echo up and down through these corridors. Now, they have become strangely silent, and the silence is all the more intense by way of contrast. Then we begin to hear a slow chanting mantrum which seems to come from a hundred different places at once, for there are literally thousands of people who participate in this ceremony and they are standing immediately in the darkness of the corridors which lead into the central temple. Now there comes some beautiful white torches which are held aloft by several great and beautiful figures of men who are carrying these torches. They slowly walk around the great central portion and place these glowing white torches in niches, so that the place is illumined very brightly, and it seems to remind you somewhat of sunlight. At the rear of this temple you will now notice there is a huge central disc of the most intensely glowing golden crystal of a far greater hue than you have ever seen; it is casting off rays of radiant yellow light from its center, outwardly. This is the symbol of Amen Ra, the God who visited the earth and Atlantea at that time.

Now, from one of the corridors there comes, marching slowly to the rhythm of the music, a group of dancing girls who are swaying to and fro; they are dressed in very gossamer white garments, and they are casting flowers about them as they weave slowly to and fro with the chanting of the music. Soon, they have encircled the great central triangle and have disappeared into the distant corridors. Almost immediately and following them comes the Peacock Priestess, herself, and she presents a very beautiful and wonderful sight. She has upon her shoulders a cloak which is made of thousands of the eye of the peacock's tail, so that it glitters and glows with the dancing blue lights of these wonderful colors which are in the feathers of these birds. Upon her head is a great jeweled crown which is shaped like the head of a peacock; her arms are encased in long jeweled feathers which seem to sweep about her like the wings of this most magnificent bird. She is dressed in the most sparkling brilliant white garments which give a wonderful contrast to the intense brilliant blues of the feathers. Coming along behind her in two different files are similarly dressed priestesses, except that they are dressed in the blue garments of the blue species of this peacock bird. Slowly, with the chanting of the swelling of the music they circle the great central pyramid, and going through a number of rather slow but intricate movements which are somewhat reminiscent of the dances which are performed in the Orient in your present day, they finally come in front of the great central disc at the rear of the temple.

Then it is that they perform the last observant rites of this dance which portrays in every detail the longing, the grief which was attendant to the departure of Amen Ra from this earth. Then finally, in one great blinding flash of light, the God himself will disappear from the earth and leave behind nothing but the still darkness of the temple, and it is so quiet you can hear the breathing of the thousands of souls who are waiting in the outer darkness, and they will begin to silently steal away in sadness for the memory of the loss of the great loved One, the Amen Ra. For, yet, it is through the peacock that they know that he still maintains and lives with them and gives them love which is renewed from day to day when His shining face steals over the mountain ranges which are to the east of this great city. And so it will be that he will fade in the gathering shadows of the dawn of each evening; and as his smiling countenance disappears beneath the planes to the West, we know in assuredness that our day will be lighted and renewed; that in the pure blazing sunshine of the mid-day we shall again come to know the strength, the unity, the courage, and the warmth of love of the great Amen Ra.

And so, for this time, my dear brother and sister, we must remain not alone, nor shall we remain separate, but with the coming days and the hours will draw to the closeness of this time and this period and cycle, where-in in this future day we shall again be reunited in some great Celestial City which surpasses even the great beauty of Atlantea; but until this time, may I bid you all, not farewell, but Godspeed. With all my love.

— Sharamute.

(The mixed emotions felt by all three here, were so intense we had to shorten contact. It was so touching to again meet our Spiritual Brother, we all cried a little.)

CHAPTER CV

The Peace of God be with you. I am the identity of the one who was known on your earth as Zoroaster, or Zarathustra. Your history will relate me to the time of something like five hundred to a thousand years before the Advent of Jesus upon the earth. While this all seems to be a great mystery to those who study the records of the earth, yet, the time does not really matter, neither does the identity of the individual as he was so called this or that, but mostly that he lived and left behind a message — a message of Truth which was given to the people of that time and place; and as it was such that those who remain firm and staunch and adhere to the flame of Zoroaster, let them be complimented for their fidelity, and let them be blessed with the consciousness and goodness which comes to all believers, whether they follow the path of any prophet, or any Avatar, so long as the pathway leads to the higher place of God.

In your previous talk and visit to an astral world with your Brother Sharamute, you were given a scene and looked in upon the Temple on an observance as a "Festival of the Peacocks", which started in Atlantea more than 16,000 years ago according to your Gregorian Calendar; and you both actively participated, or you were both there at this time when Amen Ra descended to the earth and appeared in the great Central Temple of Atlantea and proclaimed Himself as the true Son of God.

There has been much mystery in the term "who is the Son of God", and from whence did He come, and from whence did He derive His powers. Thus, these questions were answered by Amen Ra who drew the cubic upon the raised floor of the triangular shaped granite in the temple and raised therein the block of pure crystal where He placed upon it the Flame of Life, and dwelt among the Atlanteans for over four hundred days. These things I am pointing out to the reader who may not be as well versed in these facts as you, yourself, may be. There will be many who come this way and will want to have more light shed upon the various facts leading up to these events.

My own mission here with you tonight as a delegate of the Council of Twelve of which I am a member, will be such which will conduct you through the Sixth Center; and while this has been somewhat explained to you in this previous transmission, yet perhaps this, too, will bear a little more light. It was in Atlantea, with this observance of the ceremony of the arrival and departure of Amen Ra, that it was so depicted by the various figures of the Priestesses who were dressed in the raiment which was fashioned so that it resembled these very gorgeous birds. They did not have the name of peacock at that time, but were called the "Bird from Heaven", and within each feather on the tail of this peacock which has sometimes been called the eye of Buddha, actually was so colored and placed by the finger of Amen Ra that it looked like the great Central Vortex from whence the energies of God so sprang. This was the message to you and to all of the people, that while the bird was kept, it would be a living reminder of the Son — Amen Ra, as He lived and dwelt among the people of Atlantea.

I will leave any other such questions which may arise in your minds until such future day. The final and concluding chapter of this book will be very shortly concluded. The Seventh Plane of Shamballa, (Unarius), which you have been told is a Plane or Center of devotion, is not a separate planet in itself but rises in the Central Temple which is above you on the next plateau. There will be others with whom you were acquainted at one time, including Mohammed, who will conduct you through its various wonders. This huge temple on the top of this great plateau of Unarius eclipses by far and surpasses anything in beauty and wonder that you have yet witnessed. But, we will not go too far along this

1136

line at this time as we wish that it should have an entire book or a section of the book devoted to it entirely. The work here in this Sixth Center and plateau is connected as it was explained to you, as the mother of the earth planet, Venus, or as we call Venus, "Lumens", which means, in another tongue, 'Light'.

However, Venus is a beautiful planet as you know and saw in your previous visits. You found in the higher structures upon this planet that their work was devoted to what the earth psychiatrist would call psychotherapy or the healing and adjustment of the minds and souls of humans, and to educate them a little further along the pathway of spiritual light and truth, in the natural orders and conclusions of such adjustments as would be necessary to make, not only with their bodies, but that their minds and hearts may become more habitable for the great Presence of God. They were greatly concerned with the casting out of evil spirits, or obsessions, or to rescuing such mental and physical derelicts and prostitutes from the underworlds which are called the sub-astral planes.

We shall go into these great Centers and witness the wonders and the sights of the healing which is going on in these numerous Centers and the students and the teachers who are assisting the students in the studies of these concepts. There are many miracles performed here, too, just as they were performed before your eyes on Venus as well as in some of the other centers. Here, there is a higher order of integration carried on with these various orders and practices as the students, and possibly some of the teachers, may come into the terrestrial dimensions at a future day in the history of the earth or to any of the subsidiary planets which are in these various solar systems throughout the great galaxies of the universe.

The future spiritual practitioner, as he will be called in these future days, will have considerable knowledge along these lines whereby healing can take place with many of the numerous types of mental derelictions which are now considered, on the earth, almost incurable. We shall consider for a moment drug addiction. As you witnessed it from one of your programs on the TV screen, it was quite evident that by far the largest percentage of these many thousands of hopelessly addicted persons, whether or not they took treatment, usually reverted back to the state of complete dereliction. Drug addiction will be treated along the lines of other types of obsessive malformations of the psychic body, as will such things as alcoholism, sex perversions and numerous other types of very obsessive and destructive conditions with which people struggle in attempting to cure their fellowmen who have thus become so obsessed and intermeshed and entwined in the coils of these very terrible astral forces.

The chemistry which goes on in the cases of those so addicted, in the physical body as well as in the psychic body, itself, if I can use the term chemistry, is of such nature that it very seriously warps and distorts, and in some cases destroys certain centers in the psychic body, itself, so that these addicts of alcoholism, or such drugs which have been in use on the earth and in other planets, are of such nature, that we might say they are destructive to the extent that the damage is irreparable so far as the earth doctor or scientist is concerned. These persons are being taught, for future benefit and use to the earth people, how to reconstruct and reconstitute any individual who is so addicted to alcoholism.

We can also classify the habit of cigarette smoking as a somewhat milder but nonetheless venomous form of drug addiction. Because it appears to be more mild does not mean that it is less harmful to the psychic centers. The spiritual therapy and cures and rehabilitions of these unfortunate human derelicts must await such time until they can be transported into astral dimensions and their psychic bodies rebuilt and replenished from the great storehouse of God's Universal Mind Vortex. These energies sometimes take long periods of time to grow and nourish these psychic bodies, so that often an alcoholic or dope addict, if I can use the term 'dope', is not able to return or given the privilege of reincarnating to the earth in possibly periods of two to four thousand years after he has lost his physical body in the terrestrial dimensions where he became addicted to the practice of drugs and alcohol.

Nor is the subject closed with the use of drugs, alcohol, or cigarettes; there are many other types of poisons which are being absorbed into the minds and psychic bodies of many hundreds of thousands of eartheans which is all just as insidious in nature in the long run and will become just as destructive. We refer to those intemperate practices which continually detract the person's attention from the true course of life, to the vast amounts of various types of exploitation along the lines of the reactionary nature of man or to such suggestive picturizations which lead man into the coils of sexual obsessions. In fact, most anything which is of the nature which is considered the material elements of your world and time can thus be placed in this category. The man or woman who slaves his life away to create and to buy for himself the various expensive luxuries of his time and day, is only strengthening the power of the great, mad, over-all materialism as he is holding the earth on his hands and shaking it gleefully with his taloned fingers, while the blood of millions of people pour from between his fingers.

There are many of the former earth scientists and doctors who are working in this Center and who are taking the various instructions; and in some of the more advanced cases, they are in turn, teaching. One of the great scientists who will come into the domain of the earth people in the future will be in the realm of what is presently called psychokinetics or the extension of the mind forces. Man will learn to constructively use this great power of his mind and to be able to direct the great generic forces of God which stem through him into productive and useful purposes which are not necessarily of the selfish nature, but will concern man in some Universal brotherhood; and in this great Universal concept he will be cleansed and made whole from many of the ills which are at present threatening to destroy the races of mankind.

If the people of the earth are obliterated from their planet in a future day, it shall not be from the atom bomb or its use, but rather from the destructive purposes of spiritual malnutrition from which man will separate himself so completely from the idea consciousness of the creative elements of God. He will obliterate himself from the face of the earth. However, do not take this as a prophecy. It is a danger but one which is likely to pass; and I can truthfully say that it will pass to a large extent and a large degree. But we must remember that in passing will also be the passing of hundreds of millions of lustful individuals who are now attempting to live in these material dimensions with the idea consciousness of self as the predominating and most motivating power which seems to give rise to their existence. These selfish individuals will be replaced by the God-loving and man-loving individuals of the future who will understand the true nature of man and his affinity to the God Force and to the higher purposes of life; man, through his numerous cycles, is so struggling to achieve this continuity with the true spiritual expressions of his inward self.

And so, if you were to completely explore this plateau, just as would be in the case of the others, it would occupy many, many years or perhaps several earth lifetimes as you would count time on your earth calendar. The various factions are so divided to promulgate the utmost harmony and expression and in the conclusion of the numerous activities in which the student and teacher so participates with the general idea in mind that whatever this various function or teaching is, it will be so integrated and interlocked with such future earth evolutions. It is here that the future nurse or the scientist or the doctor will organize something, shall I say, of the spiritual band or a spiritual relationship with these higher orders, so that through the higher reaches of his superconscious self, he will, from day to day in his life on the earth, in a future time, so bring into the expression of this life the things which he has and is learning at this present time in this Center.

For the present at least, we will discontinue the exploration of these Centers, but before I leave you I shall tell you something more about the future visits which you will have with the great Center which is just above you. The chapters which are contained in this book will conclude with the dedication from the great Leader of Unarius Himself, He whom you once knew upon the earth as Jesus. He will personally dedicate this book and this work which you are doing to the service and to the enlightenment of mankind. He will also include in this dedication a necessary healing element which will insure and guarantee that all those who read the book will be touched in a spiritual way which will mean much to them in their spiritual progression. It will enable us here in these numerous Centers to reach out with the fingers of our love to touch these individuals kindly into such places of their psychic selves where the pain is most felt; and we can interject into these psychic centers the necessary inspiration, and healing, and comfort which will enable the individual to progress in his future evolutions. He may or he may not feel this influx of spiritual power; or, if he does, he may quietly within his own mind say, God has heard my prayer and answered it; but we know here that while it is God who answers all things, all questions or all problems, yet it must be the relationship of man to his fellow man that God will find the fullest and the highest measure of expression. So until we meet again, my dear brother and sister.

— Your brother Zoroaster.

Note:

I (Ruth) asked the guide if these great Avatars were all one personality, reincarnated over, such as Amen Ra becoming the man Jesus. The reply:

"My dear, what you ask is an age-old problem and one which we do not wish to solve in the concept of personal individuality as to who is who, and to our various names. Let us say that we are, as they are concluded in the earth histories, all separate individuals, but that we are all working from the one spiritual Logos to express the same quotient and truth and intelligence. It might be that in the similarity of this expression, some men have found the element whereby they believe all of us to be the same; yet this is not so. We are indeed all individuals, all working with the same great spiritual Logos, and while the individual concept is not the same as it is understood in the language of the earthean, yet it is a very precious and valuable condiment in our own relationship to the Immortal Father of all, and we do not wish to lose this individuality, as here in these Centers such individuality assumes what is more properly called God polarity. I hope this answers your question."

I questioned Him further regarding the phrase, 'The Son of God'. "My dear, the problem of being or assuming that any person is 'The Son of God', as He is so called, only means that in the true sense he has arrived at some distinct point of a positive polarity with this great God Force. It means that this individual would, in the terms of the average individual from the planet earth or to such similar planets, be able to see in such a person the powers of the God and thus say that he was 'The Son of God'. However, you may rest assured that every human being is a son or a daughter of God. There are no exceptions and no distinctions. It is all a question of polarity as to how or whence we achieve the certain point of relationship with the great God, so that we are able to directly express some small portion of this God Force outwardly into such form or substance as you may call miracles. Or that we may leave behind us something from which the average people of the earth may look upon the record and say that he or she was an Angel, or that he left behind him something which was of great benefit to the posterity of mankind.

Amen Ra, as he was called or proclaimed himself in Atlantea, as 'The Son of God', was not the Jesus; He came from another great spiritual Universe where he had evolved from one of the lower terrestrial Universes, and his mission in Atlantis was one which filled a very definite need and a gap of the spiritual beliefs of the people at that time. While they had instinctively realized that the sun in their sciences which was given them from Lemuria was in some way a vortex of expression of great Radiant Energy from the higher Source, as it has been explained to you, yet they were sadly in need of certain personification, for it is such that men in the lower terrestrial planes must objectify such great universal powers into idea or personifications of individuals because they lack the infinite concept of perceiving the absolute abstract. So that all great powers must in some way, for a short time, at least, in their numerous evolutions be so personified into individuals.

This also strengthens and lends some weight to the idea of the 'Son of God' concept, which has been so strongly written in your scriptures. Because there again man is struggling with his inward sense of the abstract as it is contained in the superconsciousness against a material finitism of his immediate terrestrial domain so that in such a struggle he must, for some time, so personify the great God Forces which are not personal in any sense of the word, but remain completely a part of the great abstract God; and every man so arrives at the place where he begins to understand this God and to express outwardly this great God from himself and he becomes a 'Son of God'. Until then, you are children of God.

THE

VOICE OF ELYSIUM

Clairvoyantly Received

By

Ernest L. Norman

***

The Seventh Volume of

THE PULSE OF CREATION

***

*

Published by

Unarius - Science of Life

CHAPTER CVI

My beloved brothers and sisters: First, I will bow in humble acquiescence to the honored custom of personal identity. I am known to the student of occultism as Matrea. It is a most auspicious occasion to be able to see you here in the topmost elevation or plateau of the great City of Unarius; this section is called Elysium and most properly links it with a similar astral planet which is in a slightly lower rate of vibration much like that of Venus. The trip to this planet may, or may not be made possible again in the future, depending largely upon the results and time which is taken in the exploration of this great Center Section. You were officially conducted here by — I will say it the easiest way, Zoroaster — although we pronounce it quite differently, and he officially opened, as I said, your visit to this Center of Elysium here upon the apex of this great crystal plateau of Unarius. It is this section which is devoted to those many millions of individuals who are particularly devout in their religious observances and to the various and numerous transpositions and promulgations of spiritual devotion. As you know, the priest, or the minister, or any individual who is most properly devoting his life to these religious customs and observances of his time and of his place and country is more or less under the jurisprudence or jurisdictional guidance of Elysium, so that he may be most properly functioning from this particular vibration.

However, I believe there are many who will be curious as to my identity to the periods of evolution when I lived in the terrestrial planet earth, so I shall first enlighten you somewhat into these various evolutions. While it is most proper that I have not assumed a physical body for many hundreds of thousands of years on the

1145

earth, yet, I have served in some spiritual capacity and have, shall I say, materialized into different dimensions at proper intervals of time to render whatever help and guidance I was able to constitute at that time. My previous evolutions in the terrestrial dimensions, where I actually inhabited an earth body or a fleshy frame, was over a hundred thousand years ago; and now as Ruth has read something of the history of the pyramids in China and in Central America, may I say of the pyramid in China, that I was at one time a devotee in this great temple or pyramid of learning of the ancient sciences of Lemuria and which was actually almost 140,000 years ago. This great pyramid was built under the direct supervision of the Lemurian Masters nearly 160,000 years ago, and other similar pyramids were constructed under their direction in Central America; also, in the later periods the pyramid of Giza in Egypt was constructed 82,000 years ago. I can give you these dates with much authority as I assisted and participated, not only in their dedication, but in the service in these pyramids at different times, and I may say that it is most deplorable that the present day archaeologist or scientist takes such a dim view of the quotient or element of time that he thinks a few thousand years ago means the outermost limits of what is called his archaeological science in his beliefs or of the ancient cities or civilizations of the world. He is most sadly mistaken, and we could very truthfully give him the locations of buried cities and proof of civilizations which lived almost a million years ago on the planet earth.

These civilizations were very wonderful and beautiful in their entirety and in their nature. I may add also that there have been numerous races of people who have come and gone from the planet earth, to which they came from the other planets, not only of your own universe, but the universes which are but just dimly visible in the photographic plates in the great observatories of your time. The wonders of the evolutions or civilizations in the past ages, as they have come and gone on your little terrestrial planet, are indeed most fascinating subjects to study. They are all contained in the numerous, shall I call them, museums or the great halls of learning throughout the seven different planetary Cities of Unarius; and some day most all of the archaeologists, as they are pitting their intelligence on your earth today, will evolve into these great centers of learning. They will be able to pick up the threads of these civilizations and to further explore them and so fully satisfy themselves; but this must, of course, be in a time when their minds are sufficiently illumined and broadened to the necessary magnitude where they can accept the great and Infinite Universal Mind of God in His Entirety.

Now, we shall get back more properly as your eyes — if I can call them eyes — are so focused here on the apex of this great Center on the Central Plateau; however, I may also say, before we get more deeply into this discussion that a great friend of yours will conduct you on one of your future transmissions; a Brother known as Mohammed, and he is standing by, most patiently, here with me this evening awaiting his turn. He is quite happy in the fact that he has given you some rather inspirational bits or lines of wisdom or truth which you are to presently impound in your various earth books.

Looking about you, you will see the most subtle and beautiful purple or violet radiation, and this seems to be the most predominant color of the elements of the many colors which are coming from the innumerable brilliant spectrums of pulsating radiant energy with which you are so customarily surrounded in these visitations. Now, that you are becoming accustomed to viewing these beautiful sights, you will see here some structures which are very familiar to you. The Radiant Energy has been so changed or altered from its naturally vibrant or fluid state that it has become what appears to be a solid substance which is used for these buildings. The city, itself, is laid out like a huge lotus flower with seven petals or separations with a huge Central Temple. While we have rather loosely called the whole plateau a temple, yet, it is actually a small planet all by itself because of its vast and immense size. It houses many millions of people and students who are coming and going through these great Centers. Each one of the Seven Centers or petals are properly linked to the different and relative planes of Unarius in their own specific relationship on the order of frequency or harmonic relationship or vibration as it has been explained to you. The Seventh is, of course, our own particular vibration here and relates it also to a vibration which is most suitably linked to a higher Celestial dimension which is sometimes called a Logos or one of the thirty-three Logi.

It is through this temple that many of the more fully developed individuals come and go from these thirty-three great Centers, or the 'Logi', as they have been mentioned to you in your previous transmissions. This whole plateau does vibrate or so link itself with the most spiritual essences of man's entire nature whether he is the primitive savage in the jungle who worships the spirits of the trees, or the rocks, of air, fire, or water, he is, in a most pure sense, still a devotee and so comes under the general vibrationary rate of this Center. It is in this capacity we are able to more properly serve the different orders of mankind as he finds his experience in the various terrestrial or astral worlds.

As far as my own personal part is concerned in the service in this Center, I am more or less an ambassador, if I can use this term to apply to a service which more or less renders me as a connecting link and a sort of personal purveyor or emissary from the higher Celestial structures; I frequently come and go, especially in such times or cycles which are most appropriate and which will, in due course, mean considerable in these spiritual values in interpretations to the earth people or those in the other astral worlds.

The period from 1954 to 1964 is the eleven year cycle which is most highly conducive for the transposition of the cycle of the earth into what has been generally called the Aquarian Age. It will be during these years and especially the year 1957 which is in the exact center of this period of transition, so this year of 1957 will be the one which shall be most vitally concerned with the great numbers and appearances of different spiritual manifestations and movements or critical adjustment periods in the history of the earth. Whereas on the whole, the eleven year cycle, too, will be most productive of different kinds of phenomena in political, spiritual, and scientific fields.

Going from one of these great sectional Centers to the other will be a most joyous pleasure for the different individuals, as they have been most carefully selected on the basis of their value to the earth student who will read these lines so that, all in all, there will be at least six more chapters which will be concluded with the dedication from the Central Officer Himself.

We are quite reluctant to use terminology which denotes authority as we are all in a most harmonious accord, and we relate our various activities according to our abilities; we are never challenged for the mere superficial value of these interpretations in spiritual values in our services to mankind. But rather, if we become somewhat weak, we are lent strength, and if we are most strong, we are able to lend strength to those who are not so strong. Never do we attach any personal stigma of weakness or authority to our services, but are all most grateful and humble to serve in whatever capacity we may serve, large or small. Your last visitation will be most properly conducted in the near future into the Center from whence you first started your transmissions and writings of your book which will be the Sixth Center or the one which is connected in the rate of vibration to Venus.

We do sincerely hope that none of you are confused by the various and seeming multiplicities of connections and reintegrations of these different Centers; a little careful thought as you proceed with the readings will keep you from becoming lost in a maze or a labyrinth of seeming repetitions. For these things are indeed most duly divisible according to the highest order of service which may be rendered by, not only the divisibility into most proper channeling, but a most proper over-all interrelationship and integration.

The Sixth Center here which is connected to Venus will be shown to you in one of the future transmissions wherein you will be taken into the Center and shown how the various devotees have learned to approach and understand God in a most spiritual manner through the process of spiritual inspiration and healing to their fellow man. The successive planes as they were, of Parhelion or the plane of science — and here too will be a more familiar subject to you, as you will see how the scientist learns to approach God through the test tube and the microscope, thus becoming a devotee of the most munificent of the All Pervading Intelligence; you will continue on until you have made the entire circumference. I shall not, at this time, tell you the identities of those who will come to you and lead you in these explorations or transmissions as we wish this to be somewhat of an element of surprise to the future reader; you will grant us this much leeway in promulgating the personal interest in reading the book as this will be most productive for the future reading.

In the future, after the circumference has been completed and the most proper transmissions given, you will be led to the Central Temple where the Dedication

1150

Ceremony and service will be conducted on Easter morning. Before I close I would like to bring forth a few more points of our own particular Center here, as this is the Seventh Section of this great Center which is devoted primarily to the pure and inspirational type of devotion to God in the various and numerous ways and walks of mankind, in the most numerous of his terrestrial and astral worlds. There are many priests, ministers, and spiritual leaders who have lived on the earth planet at different times who are now teaching and learning in this great Center. To name some of them would be like reading the roll call from most of the histories of the planet earth. As far as their being religious leaders is concerned, as I have said, it is also a connecting link to the higher Celestial dimensions as well as serving a connecting link to the lower astral plane of Elysium which is a planet of rest, or as it has been called the Devachan; or the spiritual world of integration for the newly migrating soul of a spiritual nature who has left the earth plane or some such similar planet. He will rest there in that Center of Elysium before he ascends here to this Center or he may, after resting, ascend into some other suitable astral world which is more duly compatible with his newly awakened spiritual state. Here in this Center are vast cities where you might wander for long periods of time and see monasteries and numerous monks. You might see convents; you might see the various cities of the Essenic orders of Ancient Greece, Egypt and Chaldea. You could also see the devotees in the cities similar to the templed cities of India. These devotional exercises and interpolations of spiritual service were constantly entered into and studied by these numerous devotees, as they were partially reliving some phase or facet of some previous life for the benefit of future study and exploration to some newly arrived group of individuals who wished to study these various methods and tenures as they had been produced in some planet like the earth. So, all in all, as this is a vast Center we can only very lightly skim over the surface and leave the rest up to the imagination of the reader in filling out some of the vacant spots which may enter into his introspection.

It will be enough, however, for him to gain a comprehensive view of our services here in the general functioning of the processes of evolution in the grand scale of ascendencies to the races of humanity who have visited the earth in different reincarnations. Now, my dear brother, I shall not keep you here longer but shall return you to your respective position on your terrestrial earth. For the future we shall be separated only by the physical form of flesh, but through our minds we will often communicate and be together. Until that day when we can be embodied in the spiritual worlds, dear ones, the abundance of God's blessings be with you.

— Matrea.

CHAPTER CVII

(Ruth smelled the fragrance of the effulgence of one of the teachers, and we defined it as being this particular one and were discussing where he lived when he was on the earth, when came this answer): It does not matter that I was Chinese or Hindu, or that I lived in the place which is known as Central America or Maya; but that I served means more. These were incarnations which portrayed in their own time and in their own sense one who can be called Dratzel. That I may have been known also by other names means little, but that I am here with you means much more. Before leaving you to go to another section of this great Center, we will take you rapidly down the great corridor which divides this Seventh Section and forms a means for ingress and egress; it is more than just a corridor as you will see that it takes you quite a little while to walk from one side to the other, walking very rapidly. It could be easily a mile in width; you see that there are many thousands of souls who are moving rapidly back and forth through this great corridor. I will not say, moving upon the surface, because we do not travel on the surface as much as we simply travel. I hope that this method does not confuse you. Now, going down this great corridor I can point out numerous sections which are actually huge dimensions, in themselves, portraying to the students and to the teachers alike, the different dimensions of inspirational devotion which goes on through many innumerable evolutions of lives in the average individual's span of existence. Here, in this Center, you will see the more modern of what is termed Catholicism which is presided over by such personages as Saint Francis of Assisi and various others who are learning and teaching the initiate in the various transpositional phases of Catholicism as it was in existence upon the earth.

Let us say, however, that none of the materialism which was portrayed by some of the priests or exponents of that period is portrayed here, but rather only in a relationship that it will mean a useful lesson for the future student in his evolution — to not participate in such materialism. As in all other great religions, Catholicism was, and still is, relegated to these materialistic influences from designing or conniving minds who would use any divine science for the purposes of self-exploitation and benefits. You might find other notable personages in the portrayal of that religion and the numerous branches of the various Protestant and reform religions which sprang from the revolt against what has been called the Holy Roman Empire; you will see these numerous priests, ministers, or bishops as they lived in their earth lives during the period of Reformation or until more recent times.

Across the corridors here you will see a great personage who is teaching in a Center or dimension which is devoted to Egyptology — a person named Hermes. There are many devotees of both ancient and modern Egyptology who are presiding in this dimension and are teaching the initiate as well as being taught by the higher Adepts who come into this Center, and so it is on down the corridor. We can mention here that this section or dimension is devoted to the past, the present and the future of Hinduism, and modern devotional lives in India and the surrounding countries of Thailand and Borneo and most dramatically displayed and kept alive — a functional order in this great Center.

Here, is another area in the ancient and modern Chinese religious systems in devotional capacities. It is most proper for me to say, at this moment, that the experience of inspirational devotion within oneself to the higher order is most cleansing and revitalizing if it is done most properly with the correct understanding and the knowledge that you are entering in and participating in the expression of God. It is your purpose in your evolution to find out this fact most dramatically, which is exploited in your numerous reincarnations, that

1154

you should never, at any time, separate yourself from the God Force or the God Expression within you. You should never set God aside and worship Him, but you should approach Him as He would have you approach Him in a living way. You are His child or His creation so that He may enter into you fully and thus will you be cleansed and revitalized and be rebuilt. This is the purpose of all of these great Centers here in this most high plateau of Unarius — to instruct both the initiate and the Adept into the most proper functioning of the integration of this Life Force. As we proceed down this great corridor, we find all the old and most ancient orders of religions, theosophical, theological, or devotional cultures which have ever existed on your own present planet, plus many of those which are within your own influence from various other Celestial or astral planets which are swinging throughout these vast galaxies of what is sometimes most wrongly called space. So it is that I have been most happy that you have permitted me to enter your sanctuary and to conduct you in these explorations in whatever small capacity that I am capable, and I shall be most happy to serve in whatever way I may in the future.

God's Blessings, Dratzel.

CHAPTER CVIII

Cheerio! May a former Britisher come in and chat a while? I am or was formerly known as William Thomson or sometimes called Baron or Lord Kelvin; I was a scientist who served humanity on the British Isles during the late 1800's and passed from this plane — as you have been reading in your encyclopedia — in 1907. This should be of importance to you as you were born in 1904, and it was 'shortly after my passing that I was able to come into your vibration where I have been assisting somewhat in the scientific endeavors as you have expressed them in your world since that time. It was in the field of science in the most advanced concepts at my time that I was able to bring into the world many useful exploitations of science which related to thermodynamics, various types of absolute temperature scales, to trans-Atlantic cables, and such things as cosmology, solar energy, etc. However, you must read your encyclopedia further to get a better idea of this. I have been chosen as the guide to show you through this Section of this great Center of Elysium at the top of the great crystal plateau of this City of Unarius; and, as has been explained to you, this is the scientific section which is connected directly with Parhelion and is the vibration in which you most normally function.

It is through the minds of these scientists here who are expressing a considerable amount of the scientific knowledge which you are giving in your classroom; I might say that I attended your class last Saturday if you are somewhat in doubt as to who it was that was giving some of the principles involved. (We had wondered.) I might say, too, that Darwin was most pleased that you got his point across. That concept has, incidentally, worried him for a long time. He has something which might be likened to a little sense of guilt since he left the earth because he did not fully explain the principles of evolution and thought you did very nobly. It only remains for the human minds to absorb the things which were given to them, and I am amazed that so much could have been given in so short a period of time in your dimension.

Now, it should be very apparent, not only to your students, but speaking generally of the world as a whole, that the earth is going through the change of a great cycle, and this is a very scientific cycle. These sciences will either create and reproduce a new race of people who are more suitably adapted to living with these higher concepts of life, or this science will surely destroy them, so the earth will have to be replanted with the new flora and fauna, new humanity in future ages after the atomic radiation has cooled. There are other numerous factions, or shall I call them more or less fear mongers, who are spreading doctrines which are somewhat falsely related to the astral concepts of some worlds, about so-called space-men who are ready to plunge in and save the world from destruction. Now, there are, of course, many entities who live in the astral worlds who are dominated by a great sense of, shall I say, 'service to humanity'; but these forces or these entities, as they represent either individuals or large groups, are, sometimes, as you have been told about the Venuseans in the lower orders, not always well-directed nor are they always well ordered. So therefore, many earth people, at your present time, are falling victim to the well-meant but misdirected efforts of these astral forces who are interjecting their philosophies or their doctrines into the minds of the earth people. To clear up this situation before we resume our exploration, I will point out to you, that, as you know, there are great numbers of huge, as well as lesser or smaller astral worlds which exist in dimensional frequencies which are above that of the earth, and hundreds of billions of people are living in these worlds. They, just as the earth, have very large scientific evolutions such as the world is now going through, and much more so, indeed, because these people are so far advanced to the earth that the people of the earth might be millions of years catching up with them. They may be in possession of certain great cosmic secrets of the transference of energy into different forms where they make various spacecraft and become little busybodies in space, snooping around in the various planetary systems and sometimes creating a large amount of havoc in the normal living habits of these terrestrial inhabitants. The normal function of people in these planets is always to assume, as you have explained, a direct evolutionary process through reincarnation to work out their problems. Any interference from outside, or interstellar, or cosmic forces, or astral relationships would be quite foreign to the nature of the terrestrial dweller, and should be completely and thoroughly ignored; or even if they are investigated they should be accepted on the basis of the merits which they possess which means absolutely nothing at all in the final analysis. As you can see, no one can be taken out of the thought patterns, as you have termed it 'his little pit of clay' which he has dug for himself. Only by his own will and own volition can he evolve or reincarnate into higher structures, which he will eventually do if he is left alone long enough. If you were to go into the hen house and disturb the chicken who was laying the egg, it would be quite likely to delay the process, somewhat, as well as give the poor fowl a serious complex for her future efforts. So it is, if I can interject this very homely comparison into our philosophies, very similar to those inhabitants of the earth, that these 'meddlers', as I call them, from these astral and cosmic worlds, are continually more or less influenced by the sense of power they have taken on from being able to go from one planet to another un-inhibited and they very often adopt very strong ego structures which makes them to a degree, tyrannical in nature.

Now, I must not be misunderstood on this point, and I shall make myself very clear, because there are very worthwhile forces who are working for the benefits of the terrestrial planets. Unarius is the group of the Seven Centers which are working with mankind for his own salvation, and there are others not so highly developed, or shall I say, astral world forces who are also working along these same channels; and these channels of endeavor are strictly through the intuitive, or in the language of the earth psychiatrist, through the subconscious inflection. In other words, through the hypcognic or in the sleep state, a person is given intuitively or within his psychic self, the necessary inspiration, the knowledge and wisdom to carry him through some particular crisis. This is es-pecially true with the world leaders, and you have seen this work out several times in political circles in the last year. These great changes or 'about faces' in the political relationships of some of the nations of the world have been inspired directly through these channels. This has a much greater effect and has a greater value in service to the terrestrial man than landing any number of spacecraft could possibly effect. In fact, one spacecraft landing visibly within sight of some metropolis would immediately panic every inhabitant of that city, and this panic would be very disastrous. Even though there have been pages and pages of saucer or spacecraft sightings, yet the average individual could not endure the sight be-cause it is rather an awesome spectacle when once it is viewed from the physical eye. The fact of the matter is, these things should be ignored to the point where you might look at them the same way you look at the animals when you go to the zoo; but you would not like to go in and play with them.

To get in with the spacecraft or to get in with that faction of people who have been distracted from their true course of life and from the solution of their own problems is another one of the little foggy spots of miasma which are sometimes encountered by individuals who get to the point where they become a little frustrated with trying to equate themselves in establishing an equilibrium with the different pressures of life which are about them. Now, we shall go directly into this huge Center which you see before you; before entering you see the all-pervading color outside is more violet or purple, yet as we go inside, this color changes or rather I should say, the feeling changes to the same vibration of color as you felt in Parhelion, which at first you thought was white but later developed into something of a brilliant cerise or a reddish tinge. Here inside, we find numerous students and teachers just as in the other Centers, some who are living here in great dormitories or buildings; they are coming and going and studying the numerous apparatus which is associated through the innumerable dimensions of man's time. There are very many wonderful things here which would be a revelation to the earth scientist just as they were to myself when I first came here, and although I had been associated with Shamballa before coming to the earth in my last reincarnation, yet, I was amazed to find that my earth service had, shall I say, quickened my mind to a point where I was now able to communicate and converse or to observe things which had been formerly out of my dimension of concept.

In one of the previous transmissions it was mentioned that one of the great dangers which shocked humanity of the earth at this time was not the atom bomb but the overproduction of the races, and the food supply would diminish to the point where synthetic foods would have to substantially replace the naturally grown foods. There is a particular field of endeavor here with which I have been connected which is most interesting and relates to insect life; now, turning from a pure scientist to something of entomology is something which I did not exactly foresee in my future from the earth. But I found, just as you were speaking Saturday night, that insects too, just as your little Charley, the amoeba, had a very definite evolution. Your present day scientist is confounded with the fact that his new insecticides very soon lose their potency, as future generations of insects develop and have within their little bodies or minds a complete immunity from new insecticides.

I have been studying along these lines for some time, and I have been looking into the cycles of the future and do say that coupled with the great sense of overproduction of humanity, man faces starvation. This could be well augmented by the insect hordes, and should science cease for one moment his battle against the insect hordes, he could be completely overwhelmed in a few years' time. It is also quite conceivable in the future, new insects will develop through the processes of evolution, (as you have been explaining to your class) with which science will be unable to cope. They may be faced with a very grave danger from having the earth completely denuded of all vegetable life from some of these great hordes of insects. I am saying these things for the future because it means that stemming up from these vast seas of negative energy, which have been generated through the living processes of the many hundreds of thousands of years on the earth, there are certain scientists who are working in other planes who are helping to develop these insect pests. There have been during the time of your earth life, on the movie picture screens, such portrayals as the Frankenstein Monster and of such a scientist who would labor in his laboratories to create such things, yet, there are certain, shall I say, scientists of the left-handed factions who exist in some of the astral worlds who are creating these same Frankenstein Monsters to let loose upon the earth or upon some other terrestrial planet as part of these experimentations. These monsters will not be in human form but will be tiny insects with wings and with stingers and little jaws and which which will munch and eat everything from the face of the earth.

I would point out to the earth scientist, too, that his greatest weapon of defense is not in the powers or solution of chemicals which he has, heretofore, used with only a moderate success against his insect pests, but we will, in the future when the time is most apropos and suitable, give to him radiant energy machines which will enable him to control these insect pests. I would like to say here, incidentally, that while I was upon the earth, I too, tried to give to mankind the theory of the Universal Radiant Energy, and was most unsuccessful. Science would not accept God as coming down through the many different dimensions as whirling Radiant Vortexal Energy. But your whole hypothesis or the structure of your science, as you are expressing it, is based primarily upon these concepts as they were given to you — not only partially by myself, but from many of the other much greater minds than my own. I, too, was an instrument in the service of these great minds when I was upon earth and trying to explain these concepts to man. But do not let that dismay you for one moment because sometimes it takes many years for the little stream of water to wear away a huge granite boulder, but the granite of obstruction which exists in the human mind is purely an element which is existing in its own time and its own cycle and so it, too, shall pass.

The Radiant Energy Vortexal Theory will be very thoroughly understood and accepted; as a matter of fact, part of science in the near future years which are ahead of you, and if you can take any small part of satisfaction in this statement, then rest assured that you will have the 'last smile'; for I can state, with the utmost sincerity and the utmost sense of truth, that what you are teaching, as well as what I am learning here in these dimensions which are above the earth, as they have been explained to mankind in your writings and in the transmissions, are actual truths and actual facts which so exist. It only remains for the eyes of mankind to be opened inwardly instead of so much outwardly, that he will be able to perceive these things in their entirety.

Getting back to these Radiant Energy machines, there is in store for mankind in the terrestrial dimensions in the future hundred years or so, what we call cosmic generators, that is, they are machines which can be set on the tops of high mountains which will 'tune in' the great Magnetic Lines of Force which are stemming out from the Great Central Vortex of the Universe. Atomic power will be as obsolete as is the steam engine in your day and your time of diesels. In this future day, atomic powers will be just as obsolete as a bonfire. The huge cosmic generators will light and heat and completely power the world of the future. This same type of cosmic generator will exist in the flying machine of the future and will transport man from planet to planet. It will also be in the nature and in the dimension of this same cosmic energy machine which will enable man to, at least temporarily, change the different vibrating frequencies of all his known atomic structures. Then he can create new atoms which will compound metals or materials which are more suitable for the spacecraft which he now does not possess.

If he should go out into space in his present craft which he is trying to develop as a rocket propelled missile he would be very quickly destroyed when he arrived outside of the protective envelope of the earth's atmosphere.

The average scientist does not know that even one tiny little speck of cosmic dust which is about as large as the head of a pin could destroy any spacecraft upon impact and there are literally millions of these tiny particles through space in all directions. Even the smaller particles which he calls cosmic energy could, in a very short time, reduce any of his present known alloys upon the earth to powder, simply because they exist in frequencies and dimensions which would be so destructive to the atoms of this metal; his metals would simply disappear in a short period of time. I would also interject here, a word of caution, that the future spacecraft will have to be constructed of metals which have a vibration rate or frequency which is not in the dimension of these cosmic energy particles, and that they will be most properly insulated by an energy shield which will surround them. All spacecraft have this shield, and that is what helps to give them the appearance of fire or a brilliance as they pass from one stage of progression to another because, in the utmost limits of their speed, they look like a white streak which is going through the sky.

Also, I would say to the earth scientist that his terminology about time is obsolete and out-of-date and 186,000 miles per second is as old-fashioned as grandma's knitting needles. He will find in space that his time does not exist in that particular quotient; he will have to develop an entirely new mathematical system which is based entirely upon a cycular pattern which he does not now possess; and this will rob his present day mathematics of much of its value. One word more about these various types of goings on about the spacecraft reportings and writings with which you have come in contact; and I thoroughly agree with you, as I have contacted your mind in reading these reports, that some of the terminology or nomenclature which is used to describe such scientific apparatus is rather crude and smacks of charlatanism. There will have to be new names as well as new machines invented. The language of the future will not be in vocabulistic systems as you now know it on the earth plane. Language, like mathematics, will become inadequate in the future day and future evolutions and will largely pass from the existence of the earth people. These things I can truly predict as I have seen them on other planets which have gone through these same principles and these same evolutions. I have talked with the people — using the word "talked" rather loosely, as one does not talk with, as Meng Tse said, a loose flapping piece of flesh in the mouth — we speak directly from the mind where nothing is hidden. There is really not much which I could add or show you in this great Center at the present time which could be acceptable to the present dimension of the earth scientist; there are different developments in the scientific world which are entirely beyond the realm of concept of any existing scientist as he dwells upon the planet earth. Such things will have to wait their proper time and their proper place in the evolution of the world, and when we say, "wait", we are using the term rather loosely here, too, for time is in an entirely different concept of interpolation or integration, as it has been somewhat explained to you in the past pages.

May we say to your students, do not expect to understand these abstractions in your terrestrial dimensions, but only try to arrive at the threshold whereby you will know that these things can and do exist in a completely new way and new world, which is, at your present mental stature completely unfathomable. The earth man's mind functions as a terrestrial agent entirely from a terrestrial plane, and when I am speaking of these things I am pointing to the average individual as he lives upon the earth plane. There are very few people who have the power to consciously levitate themselves from their consciousness as you do and to contact the higher Forces and Intelligences where these things can be brought somewhat into consciousness of other individuals.

Now, I do believe it would be best if we would return you to your respective position that you may take up your life in the usual fashion although your life is not in the usual way which is at present being expressed by the average earth person. Do not become discouraged but let the Torch of Unarius, as it is the Flame of Life, always lead you up the Pathway toward the Altar of Infinite Wisdom, and to the All Pervading Graces of God's highest Intellect. Until we contact you again, we shall be ever in your Superconsciousness.

— William Kelvin

CHAPTER CIX

Dear Ones — I am so glad to be with you this evening. I am the identity of Carrie Jacobs Bond, and am most happy to greet you from this great plane of music, drama, art, and literature here in Unarius. If you recall some time ago in your former residence, during the early summer months, I made contact with Ruth and was able to impress her with a few lines which came to my mind at that time, and thus it was that we began to open up the channel with her, so that it brings us up to this present moment where I am with you again here in this great Center of Unarius, which is devoted to the inspirational arts as they are connected to the great central planet of Muse and the vast city of Coralanthus which you formerly visited in one of your other books. Here, like all the other Centers, is one which is primarily devoted to integration and leadership in various fields. If you have studied my personal biography on the earth, you will know that I had rather a terrible time through ill health and in many ways before I was able to bring to the world some of the song and music which I felt within me and which was part of the harmony of the great Consciousness of God. The future student should remember a most important point — that in learning wisdom or knowledge from any astral plane or such Center of Unarius — he would be very wise indeed if he would also carry a full measure of wisdom in the capacity of the most vital and essential integration of leadership. It does one small good to learn or to feel the innermost expression of God working through him, if he cannot express this outwardly to humanity and share this great inspiration with his fellow man.

About the world today, just as there have been in so many hundreds of thousands of years of earth history, the talented youth of your country of America, as well as in the foreign countries of the world, are literally dying unrecognized, thus, bringing a great sorrow into their hearts which is indeed a heavy burden of karma. It is also a strange paradox in America today that those seemingly with the least talent are sometimes the most successful in expressing some very retrograde or a blatant form of music or poetry to such inspirational arts. As in their case, I would be very loathe to participate in such expressions. They are indeed purely the teachings of the lower astral realms wherein those who are dedicated to the destructive purposes of their own selfish desires are seeking to coerce and intimidate the youth of America, for it is quite obvious that America has assumed leadership in many fields. The new age shall be built from the foundations of the democratic interests in humanity as are expressed in America today.

Before I proceed further with my little discussion, I would mention that there are many illustrious persons here with me who are assisting in this transmission, and your own guide, God-father Mohammed, is here with me and is most anxious for the time in which he will personally conduct you into the ceremony of the Easter festival where you will hear the words of our Most High Leader. There are also other well-known artists and poets as well as musicians who are here with me; one who is called Franz Schubert, and you were just playing his most beautiful rendition on your stereo recorder.

But, let us continue into something of the view of the innermost dimensions of this great Center which is dedicated to teaching the student who has gained some background in his inspirational art so that he may migrate to some earth plane, as he wishes, to carry some of this very important Mind Force with him. Franz tells me — and it is common knowledge of course — in passing at a very early age from the earth plane that he very prolifically scribbled his music upon paper bags, upon the wallpaper of his room, and even upon the linen in the cafes where he ate his meals so that he was completely exhausted spiritually at a very young age, and the life force within his body was disconnected. He simply had no more to give; he had used up his life in a few year's time.

There is also another illustrious person named Handel here with us and several other composers who have lived at different times upon the earth. I personally feel very small and insignificant along side these many illustrious minds and intellects who have given so much to the enjoyment of the races of humanity upon the earth at different times.

This great Center, like it was in Coralanthus, is of the rosy pink or coral shaded vibration and is very pleasing to one's eye and to the general feeling in which one seems to be constantly in tune with some great permeating or radiating force which seems to come from within and without. Of course, this is the God Force which has been described to you so many times. Here, in this great Center there are many wonderful and beautiful dwelling places, and it is not crowded as one would expect.

I am most interested in some of the artistic trends (shall I call them) which will quite likely be manifest in the future days of the earth's history in some period of time in a hundred years or so. I have been looking at some of the homes which the architects of that time are now studying here, and will bring into your world the various arts as they will be expressed. Of course, my greater interest is primarily music, but the homes are most beautiful and they shall be constructed upon the earth of translucent plastic materials; or they shall be almost completely of a glass nature where one can look out upon the surrounding landscape. Yet, these sheets of glass-like walls will be of polarized materials so that none of the occupants are deprived of their privacy, nor, will the strong rays of the sun penetrate into the house to fade the beautiful tapestries and carpeting which I see displayed upon the floors and walls.

The furniture, too, is most beautiful and not like the clumsy wooden furniture which is in general use on the earth today. It shall be covered with surfaces which are suspended in air or air cushions. The kitchens where the housewife is supposed to cook will actually be chemical laboratories of a push button nature where the foods will come out untouched and unseen, and merely ordered, you might say, by pushing a certain button which will set a chain of robots to action. If I were to describe all of these things to the various feminine readers who are interested in culinary arts of your time, they would indeed be most amazed at what I have seen; and should I come back to the earth at that time, I would most certainly like to have one of those kitchens to prepare a little snack occasionally. There are many other wonderful and beautiful things here to see which will come into usage in the earth in a future day.

I can definitely see the mad race to oblivion as far as the automobile industry is concerned. These millions of iron monsters and juggernauts, which are killing thousands of people every year and polluting the air with fumes, will give way to new and wonderful vehicles of travel and to other means of communication which will render it unnecessary for the person to travel about.

Art, in itself, as it is known in the period of the Renaissance in Europe, while it was primarily devoted to its age and time and succeeded to a tremendous state of perfection by many of the high Masters, shall only be seen in the most ancient archives in the museums of your future world. The new art of the future will actually be done with an electronic brush which will be portrayed by the dweller of the future home. He will be able, by pressing a button and turning a dial, to bring into the room the various vistas and distant horizons in some sort of TV like apparatus which will be shown in full color and view upon the the wall of his dwelling. He will be able to communicate from city to city and see persons or groups in just such fashion in a very highly developed type of TV service, which is unlike any of the crude apparatus in use on the earth today. I have seen all of these wonderful things and many more, and I can assure you that the world, while you may think it is beautiful today, and very wonderful, will be a thousand times more so in the future.

You will not even see the common leather shoes which you now wear because leather will give way to very durable and wonderful synthetic materials which breathe much more freely than does leather, and will outwear leather a hundred times, and will be much more comfortable. Likewise, natural fibers will entirely give way to very artistic and beautiful clothing which will be constructed, not only from different types of plastic materials which you call spun glass, but will also embody many new types of synthetic fibers about which you know nothing today.

Yes, indeed, the world of tomorrow will be a very wonderful and beautiful place. In fact, the man two thousand years from now will have very little of his intestinal tract left. It shall, as the scientists say, metamorphose completely because he will imbibe food through the capsule method more than he will by taking the large bulk quantities as he does at the present. Yes, it is quite possible that man will go through a very wonderful state of evolution upon the earth and that you may look for most anything to happen in the future should you come back in any of your periods of reincarnation.

One more situation which I would say is that man should learn very thoroughly to control the birth rate of the nations of the world; and would he use the same system among humans as he is now using with his cattle, and with his dogs and horses, in that way he would be able to produce a super race of people. While this may seem a violation, at the present time, of certain inalienable rights as they are called in your Constitution, yet, wisdom of these things will become apparent through the passing of years and shall supplant the old gross ignorance with which the average person has surrounded himself in his regard to certain respects or rights, because it is not logical for people to breed a race of inferior humans and cast upon society thousands and millions of derelicts and pieces of wreckage of humanity. These things I have seen and many more which will come to pass in the future.

This is a most beautiful place and I am very happy and contented here, yet, I know that there are greater things to accomplish. Perhaps someday, in some future time, I may come back in a way for which I was not formerly fitted in my last incarnation upon the earth.

Here, it is warm and beautiful; the air is filled with radiance and music and there is a continual feeling of affinity and oneness with some great and beautiful force which is flowing within one. You can also go most anywhere you wish and attend concerts and various other highly developed cultural expressions where humanity is flourishing in a way and in a degree which is beyond the imagination of the earth dweller.

But, until such future time, my dear ones, I will come to you and especially to Ruth. I am very fond of her; she should persist in kindness and in temperance in all things that she does for these things are truly of the spirit. If she persists she shall be so richly rewarded for her tree of life shall bear the fruits of Infinite Wisdom. Until such future time, this is Carrie Jacobs Bond.

Goodbye, Dear Ones.

CHAPTER CX

The top o' the morning to you! But please don't expect me to talk in the Irish brogue even though I was once called St. Patrick on the earth plane — about 350-400 A.D. It is my own private little witticism which I like to share with many people, and one which, very often, would cause a loyal Irishman to go into a fighting mood were he to know that his 'Patron Saint' was not actually an Irishman. I was the son of a Roman Nobleman and was born in Italy in the county of Ceverns. As my father served the Roman Empire as a judge and was quite wealthy, I, at the tender age of seven became a victim of some abductors who were going to hold me for ransom. However, the kidnapping (I believe this is the right word) caused such a furor that these ruffians fled for their lives and were forced to take me with them where they fled over land and by way of the sea, until I finally arrived in Ireland and was sold into slavery.

Now the Irish at that early period of their growth were a very primitive lot of people; most of them were unspeakably filthy and dressed in the skins of wild animals. They worshipped the spirits of the rocks and trees, of air, fire, and water. Their houses were nothing more than wattled huts. The person or family for whom I served as a slave boy was in a little better position; they had a better house which they called a castle. However, it was anything but a castle; it was composed mostly of logs and crude masonry work and was several times larger than the usual run of houses. Well, after a period of time I grew to detest the whole place, and finally, after some time, I escaped and stowed away in a ship which was bound for the continent of Europe where I finally wound up and entered into some parochial school and later went into some of the schools which you might call the universities to acquire my education. Then I finally became a Bishop in the Roman Catholic Church, but I always remembered the poor backward people of Ireland living in their skins and in their filth. Then taking some of my colleagues with me, we migrated to Ireland where we succeeded after a great deal of effort, in building some schools and churches and proceeded to rather clean the place up a little. For this I was called the Patron Saint!

Now, the story about my killing all the snakes is quite untrue. The Irish at that time, had a vast herd of pigs which overran the landscapes. Pigs were always hungry and would eat anything edible including snakes. So, finally snakes ceased to exist in Ireland, but this is enough about me.

Let us go on up into the next plane or dimension of visitation in Unarius, and do you know, if you will pardon us, we have not given you a name for this big city as yet! You may call this — and I am well versed in Latin — 'Septenius', which means seven-sided or seven different plateaus or elevations. It will be a convenient name for you. As we enter this third plane of this great city which is linked to Aurelius or the plane of philosophy, and as you have looked about you, a few moments, you see it is quite like the others in many respects; but, I believe the descriptions here have been a little neglected, so we shall go into some of these elements a little more thoroughly. We shall begin walking down this great thoroughfare which could be called the latin word of Esplanade, or the central thoroughfare. Now, you have heard the stories of 'Heaven with the streets of Gold' and in looking at your feet you will see that you are literally walking on a carpet of the purest crystal which glows like gold. This is the basic gold color of the crystalline structures or the deeper orange shades which are sometimes associated with this particular plateau.

Looking off to each side for perhaps a distance of a thousand feet each way — if we can measure it in your earth measurements — you would see that the edge of this great street is lined with very beautiful tall stately trees which look like the ones you saw on Venus. Their huge tapering trunks are of the purest transparent brown crystal and they are glowing and glittering. Looking up into the canopy of branches and leaves which tower several hundred feet into the space above, you will see that each tree bears a marked difference; and while they are somewhat all synonymous, yet, each one portrays a different type or character. The trees, just as all vegetation, grows with its own individual expression or life force within itself so that it portrays, not only its own character, but takes on an individuality which is so common among all things here. They are much more closely connected with the God Force. So, you might say, while we never tend these trees, nor do we plant them, yet, they spring into existence in their well-ordered places and dimensions as part of the continuity of this whole divine scheme where all things are so working out in a much more highly evolved integrated fashion. Trees evolve in these dimensions just as do humans or any other species that you might find of the earth plane, just as you found in landscaped gardens in other cities, or that they grew luxuriantly in somewhat of a more natural state. They are all, in themselves, depicting different stages of their evolution.

Going down this great street, you will find that it is regularly bisected by other smaller radiant streets which lead into the central part of this great crystal cone. Looking on either side of the streets you will see the wide parkways in which there are huge buildings, all formed of the same orange-hued brilliantly sparkling gem-like crystal energy substance. These buildings, too, all have their individuality of character. Some are reminiscent of the old Gothic cathedrals or the various structures as they existed in the universities on the earth, or they may look like the same types of institutional centers of learning in other terrestrial dimensions. Again, they may bear a very strange and remarkable futuristic — if I can use this term — feeling there with you; and if you go into these various buildings you will see that, here, the many students have come from the other different planes of the great teaching centers to combine within the things they have learned, something of the necessary mind force in a philosophical nature which will give added strength and character to their expression on your earth or to such other suitable earth incarnations into which they are to evolve in the future.

I have been looking over the transcripts of your previous transmissions, and I believe there is one little point here which is not quite clear to you or to sister; that is in regard to reading the akashic records, and I would like to clear this point up for you to better acquaint you with the workings of this most valuable science. First, we will consider the average individual who has not yet evolved into a somewhat spiritual state of evolution; and you are well acquainted with the psychic structures and wave forms, the various implantations of these psychic happenings in his life, and how they reside in the psychic body as malformation of wave form structures. These are the key elements in the reading of the akashic as this individual has not yet arrived at the place where it would be likely that he has visited any of the planes of Unarius; therefore, he has not yet written any of his akashic in those little golden-leafed books which you saw in Parhelion and in other planes. So, you are not likely to get anything from his akashic which would in any way relate him to such excursions into these higher

dimensions. You would be given, through the association of the various personages with whom you are
working in these spiritual worlds, the word and picture
forms as they were interpreted to you from the key
structures of the wave forms. This is similar to that
which takes place in your radio set and is called rectification. That is, the high frequencies of energy come
into your mind through various processes of spiritual
integration and force. They are so reformed as to convey a picture or a continuity or a sequence of events to
you. I hope this makes this concept a little more clear
to you.

Now, the other type is what we will refer to as the
advanced soul who has made his excursions and has
been learning some form of wisdom in the higher centers, and while he may or may not be comparatively
advanced, yet, he has written in the little books what
he has already done which has been worthwhile, or
that he may have suffered severe psychic shocks in
trying to transfer his wisdom into the lower astral
worlds or into the terrestrial worlds. He will also include in these little writings the things he hopes to
do in the future and which are in the plans, or, shall
I call it, his itinerary of his future reincarnations.
This is a type of akashic which is much more easily
read simply because the book pages or events are
flashed into your mind and do not require the process
of rectification. This will explain to you why it is so
much more difficult for you to read the akashic of the
less highly evolved personages with whom you have
come in contact in the past few months. This was
true, not only because the events in their lives have
been of less serious consequences, but also that they
have made only the wave form indentations or structures in their psychic anatomies which must be suitably
rectified and which is a process that is rather haphazard, even at its best circumstance.

A few words on this and we shall proceed. If you remember the first crystal radio set which you constructed back in the early 1920's had a tiny bit of galena crystal, and these little crystals, as you know, all possess very wondrous qualities in converting energies into wave forms. This is the rectification process about which I spoke a few moments ago. It means that the supersonic vibrations are stepped down in their frequency to a rate which is understandable in the terms of frequency integration into your own mind. You must remember that the processes of thinking in your mind involves the charging and discharging of electrical currents through the brain cells and these electrical impulses all have their own wave forms or wave shapes, just as these wave shapes are oscillating in your psychic body. It is the same process except one is taking place in your brain cells and the other process takes place in the psychic anatomy. So, you see there is no difference except in the realm or dimension in which these functions take place. These concepts will bear much study.

We are also extending to you unanimously here from this Center and sharing with you the joy and ecstasy of the several events which have transpired here within your consciousness in the past few days. We are very earnestly striving here with you to bring other things into the conclusion of your lives wherein you will see the fruit being borne on this great spiritual tree of interpretation, that in the future days, you will not indulge yourselves in personal recriminations and say, "Well, perhaps I could have done a little better had I pushed a little harder." You both are doing quite well and your persistence will win out as there are some very strong and highly developed Spiritual Forces behind you, as you well know by this time.

So, we all extend to you our heartiest and most heart-felt congratulations in your new consciousness and your new awareness. We would also like to point out to you that Saint Francis of Assisi is both your personal guide and moderator and will be for some time to come. He will lend a considerable amount of spiritual strength, and shall I call it atmosphere about your humble little dwelling so that all things which come and go about you must be of a very spiritually developed nature. They will cease to have the hum-drum qualities of the mundane existence, and you will be continually buoyed up and lifted by the Presence of Spirit not only from your minds but it shall radiate from the windows of your little home into the far corners of the world. So, my dear brother and sister, tomorrow, as you know, is the celebration of this patron 'Saint' of Ireland who was called Saint Patrick, and I was most happy to come into your dwelling tonight and share with you my own private little joke that St. Patrick is not an Irishman. So, dear ones, I hope that our description of this great plane has been a little more adequate, that it fulfills a little more of the rightful expectancy which you might associate with the great Celestial Mansions. We are all waiting to serve you.

— Your good friend, Pat.

CHAPTER CXI

It is with great joy and pleasure that I can again greet you, and although I have been gone from the earth but a few years, yet, circumstances are such that I can return through this way of communication and may assist you in some of the writings for your book. For my identity, I fell by the assassin's bullet in my garden in India and was known as the Mahatma Gandhi. Do not expect me to speak in any language other than English because I was educated in England, and I will use that language even though this must all be a part of those who have spoken before; so I will bow gracefully to precedent. We are to guide you to the planet Elysium tonight. I have been so enthusiastic here in being able to return to Unarius for a while; we are to return to the planet Elysium, and we shall write some of the final chapters in your history book from this wonderful planet which is part of the great ring of the spiritual worlds which are swinging around in the universe or the void about you. I have been resting rather easily and conducting such works as were suitable in the nature of spiritual guidance from this planet of Elysium and only returned to the Centers of Unarius for the 'Holy Week' observances, as they are so integrated with the time and place of the cycles of transmission with the earth people. As you know, this is the 'Holy Week' of the Avatar Jesus and His Mission upon the earth which culminated in his crucifixion. Now, I think that is sufficient introduction for myself as my own biography is quite well-known and needs no repetition.

In fact, I was with you the other evening when you looked in on something on the magic tube which you call the TV screen which showed some of the grounds and places of my old home in India, so you know something of this time and circumstance and place. It was my great honor and privilege to be of service to the people of India. My only regret is that I did not go completely far enough into the future to set up a sufficiently formed government which would render the inflow or influx of Communism impossible. I would issue a word of warning here that has been issued by others who have preceded me; India is indeed in a grave condition. The danger of Communism is indeed much more apparent today than ever. Although there is a smoke screen in what is called the Near East, Egypt and Arabia or such places as are eventually in the calendar of dates which have been set by the great dragon, as Kung Fu calls it, to conquer that part of the world; but this only after India and many of the other latitudes on my own world, such as Thailand and other places, shall be conquered by these invading hordes of pagans. It shall not be easy, of course, because we know the natures of these peoples are just as they are found in China. My people are likewise very strongly steeped in the traditional religions of the past, and even though there may be a superficial communistic government set up yet, you may rest assured that it will not change the hearts and minds of these people.

Now, that you have begun to see clearly, you have been seeing this beautiful planet of Elysium which seems to be floating like some sort of a huge rather violet-colored glove of iridescent energy or some beautifully colored ornament such as you might find on a Christmas tree in a Christian home at Christmas time. We are approaching this planet very rapidly with the speed many times in excess to that of light. You will soon be very safely and firmly walking upon the surface of this planet, and we shall immediately go, as you have now found yourself, into a great temple which is very strangely like one which you saw on your magic tube (TV). This planet incidentally, which I have so failed to mention, is one which is devoted purely to a sort of spiritual resting place or a place of further spiritual exploitation to those individuals who come, not only from the earth, but from similar terrestrial planets. These souls are all very devoted to some religious expression, whether it is something with which you are familiar on your earth surface, or whether it is one of the religions which exist in a remote planet in another solar system. So to go through this great Temple of Buddha which you see before you and to stroll about this great city and this planet would reveal, likewise, not only all of the religions of your world as they have existed in the past down into the most distant halls of antiquity, but you would also see structures which were very foreign to anything which you had ever seen depicted in your history books. The purpose here in these Temples and in these numerous places of worship is one whereby the various souls who come from these remote planets may continue on for some time in their regular inspirational services, or they are devotees to some cult and may continue on in these efforts without serious psychic shock. They must be gradually placed in such a position whereby other truths and other paths of Infinite Wisdom can begin to illumine their minds so they will be some- what freed from these dogmatic practices in order that they may begin to conceive; for while such religious observances do have great value in certain evolutions of life, in the development of man's own individual soul and progress, however, he must also realize that the day will come in his evolution when these things need to be supplanted to a large degree and extent by the inward processes of enlightenment. He must learn that true illumination comes, not from autosuggestive practices which give rise to various sacrificial ceremonies, or to the burning of the pots of incense, to the hundred and one thousand numerous and different spiritual interpretations which exist in all levels and walks of life — not only upon the earth and in so many other worlds which we know about; but rather, illumination comes from the Innermost Consciousness. Here, we must also lend particular emphasis to those who have been somewhat fanatically steeped in these traditional practices, for these people quite naturally remain in these positions of worship much longer than those who are much more mildly inclined. So, that ever and on they become illumined in the innermost reaches of their own souls. True spiritual illumination must always come from their relationship as it is called 'from within' which actually means that through the scientific principles which have been explained to you, the individual is linked up to higher and higher Forces, or to more spiritual dimensions and interpretations of life. This is what is called the inward illumination because it must not and cannot come from the external things around you. The position of the earth mind is such that he must always see something coming from some direction, but this is not necessarily so as it exists in God's own Mind; for all things exist both internally and externally simultaneously. While man in a terrestrial position sees all things coming to him externally, yet, the most subtle essences of God's pure nature, which is the very foundation and basis for the existence of all things, must ever come from an unseen source which is called "That which is Within".

As you look about you into these wonderful and beautiful temples and various churches, they somehow seem to remind you of some of the edifices which you have seen in your cities about the surface of the earth, and indeed they may be somewhat exactly the same as these edifices are so constructed of this pulsating Radiant Energy of God's Nature. They are, indeed, very beautiful and they fit in with the general appearance of the whole world which is about you. These people whom you see walking about you, too, present somewhat of a strange appearance, quite unlike some of those whom you have been accustomed to seeing in other centers of the great Unarius. They seem to be less alert and many of them seem to be rather walking in their sleep and, indeed, this is so because they have not yet reached the point where they can see as freely about them as you do. Many of these people you see moving in and out of these great churches and temples still believe they are worshipping upon the surface of the earth. They have not realized they are, shall we say, 'dead', or that they have passed on into another spiritual dimension. Gradually, however, the great Energy Force of God's Mind shall seep through into these blank faces and illumine them from within, so they too shall be ready for some initiation and pass on into another spiritual world which is more suitable for their progression and their eventual reincarnation into a higher material status of life. Thus it is always so with these things.

I would like to interject something here of a more personal relationship and of the incense which was detected by Ruth. This means the addition of the Fourth Archangel to the Spiritual Band which is now working in your dimension, and you shall hear from Him personally in the future.

For the balance of the week, we are humbly observant in your position in life that we too are most anxious to continue on with the work; and while this book is, in itself, very important, it could very easily be but the forerunner to even greater works in the future should it be shown that all problems of the physical world about you, either internally or externally, are so compromised or placed in such a position that they do not impede the inflow of spiritual Wisdom. There are many indications about you, as you have realized, that there are other spiritual organizations which we are jointly concerned with in bringing into the world some of the spiritual evolutions which man must go through in the next coming hundreds of years; cycles that will bring him into closer relationship with the true spiritual Forces of his nature.

To America — the world can truly look forward in the future for guidance in this spiritual evolution. For this purpose, America was so conceived and dedicated from the higher spiritual planes. I am sorry we must return you to your position on the earth, but we will await your first opportunity for future contact. your Brother in service.

— Gandhi.

CHAPTER CXII

Thou hast watered my sheep, yet not from the water
which is found in the well or the stream
But is the Water of life which cometh in abundance
from above
Thou speaketh the Word, and the Word is God
yet it is not the word which casteth the
shadow wherein each man standeth and
trembles
Thou createst for each man the vision of the God
not as he who ruleth the lightning
nor cometh with the flame of sword
But he who defineth within each man the purpose
of life, and that he ruleth not with the
temper nor with the tempest
But tempereth all things with Wisdom
and bindeth all things together with
His Love
For thou see-est not with the eye of the pagan
or the Lord who see-eth with the eye of
idolatry
or worship with the carnal lust of the
world
But discerneth with the eye of Spirit
For in these things and with the infusion of
this Mind
and this eye and this spirit which cometh
And yet is withineth all man.

So he hath truly spoken of these things
For canst not one say who has been without all
these things
Yet must awaken as the child to the new day
or cry like the newborn babe
Who must suckle the breast, for always does

man yearn and long
for the return to the place of Spirit
Where he truly discerneth all things
That he see-eth all light and that he casteth
no shadow
nor live in its trembling.

(Archangel)   - Uriel

Greetings, dear ones — and Ruth, I have heard her speak many times lately, "Where is Moses?" So, here I am, or at least as much as remains after many thousands of years in these spiritual dimensions! The purpose of my visit to you is to enlarge, somewhat, the perspective of this great spiritual world of Elysium to which you were brought previously by Brother Gandhi; and so I, too, shall show you another one of our activities here in this Center. We are particularly busy at this time with the observance of the Holy Week or the Easter Festival which is taking place upon the earth. This, as you no doubt know, means that the earth has come into conjunction with certain great spiritual lines or, shall I say, magnetic force which enables us to assist in that inflow of Infinite Spiritual Wisdom and inspiration into the minds of the earth dweller at this time; and so we, or at least those who are so vitally concerned with the earth, take full advantage of this opportunity which happens only at a comparatively few times during the year, to give as much of this Spiritual Power as possible to the people.

As your Bible will tell you, the figure of Moses led the children of Israel through the wilderness, and as such a personage, set up a great dogmatic system of fundamentalism for literally millions of people upon the earth; so, after coming into the spiritual consciousness, I was immediately confronted with, and became aware of, the fact that I had led millions of people somewhat astray from the true pathway of life.

Now, this may seem quite strange to you who are used to worshipping God in the synagogues, in the churches, and in the temples; but may I point out this fact to you, that man in his many evolutions must learn to eventually understand God as the Infinite God who works from within every individual and is a part of each person. As we have determined that in man's creation, he is but a step removed from the beast and coming into that part of his evolution where God enters into his life cycle, therefore, his first contact with these Spiritual Forces, which he later learns to call God, is determined largely through the spirits of the earth, air, fire, and water. This he personalized some way as vague spiritual forms. Later on he may enter into such worships in churches, or synagogues, or temples. Here again, God becomes personified in some vague way in which he is not quite yet factually able to determine. Should any individual at any time stop his evolution or progress at some such point, he will become very firmly entrenched and steeped in these dogmatic ways of fundamentalism and so impede his spiritual progress. It is for this purpose that Elysium here functions in these great classrooms, in these teaching centers, so the various and numerous hundreds of thousands of the more firmly entrenched devotees shall have these very firm thought convictions removed from their minds and learn something more of the Infinite and inward way in which God works. Fundamentalism in any form, if it supersedes certain normal values of relationships, becomes an obsession which is just as destructive as any of the lower spiritual entities which may enter into his consciousness. As I said, this may sound strange to you that I am actually teaching people *not* to worship God in a temple or a church, but rather to learn that He is part of each individual. This is a paradox, for I taught many people to worship a God who was terrible and who was also loving and kind!

At this time we shall continue our exploration through Elysium into this great Center which you may call, for practical purposes, Devachan, which is really some sort of Heaven to those who worship God in this manner. Now, upon your earth you have many systems of integration or correlationship such as the Red Cross which dispenses food and help to various needy persons upon the earth. Also, you have your immigration service which functions to screen certain persons before entering America. We, too, in the great spiritual planes between here and Elysium maintain many such centers of integration wherein various persons are screened through different processes to determine exactly what is best needed for them at the moment. Some of these integrations have filtered into earth concepts through numerous books or pamphlets which were published. We, here, take care of such persons who are filtered through to us and sent to us who are actually people of very strong character and personages of such caliber as could be very useful and could advance in their evolution to a very marked degree except for the one impediment, namely, that they have become very firmly entrenched in these various demagogic ways of expression.

I might point out to you a very specific example of a man called Billy Sunday, who became a revivalist upon the earth and led many people down that sawdust trail toward oblivion. It is not the purpose of man to learn of God through any hypnotic processes of mind, and in separating himself from God, so that he must worship God, he dismembers himself. We here in Elysium, were most anxious that Billy Sunday could be brought to us for this corrective therapy. Unfortunately, however, he was of such strong disposition that he returned to the earth, and he is now psychically in complete control of another person named Billy Graham. So that many millions of people will actually be detoured away from their true path of spiritual progression by the infliction of the subservient position in their mentalities. They have become subservient to this God rather than a factual integrated working part of Him.

Now, that your eyes have become accustomed to the planet which is about you, and to this great city, as you were formerly with Gandhi in a great Hindu Temple in the immediate environment thereabout, we find ourselves in one of the great centers which is devoted to teaching. At first, when some subject is brought to us, or comes by his own will, he will come and go into the numerous

1191

temples which you saw on your previous visit. He is very firmly devoted to his previous thought patterns of worshipping God, so that he shall find in the pulpits or the various teaching capacities of these churches and temples, the numerous priests which he has known in previous evolutions upon the earth. However, these priests are merely disguises and, while he may adhere to a large extent to what he had learned upon the earth in his own mind, these things resolve as word forms which he can accept only as he believes them. Throughout all of these word forms which come into his mind as he listens to these priests, there also comes an added ingredient which is spiritual awakening and consciousness, as spiritual power which will gradually dissolve these very firmly entrenched thought patterns with which he has become associated in his worship practices, so that very soon he will find a distaste or a dislike for his previous ways of worshipping God. He will become conscious that there is a new way to learn of this great mysterious Force which created him and which is infinitely superior to him in every way. He shall also become aware of the fact that he must *integrate* himself *with* this great Force or Power.

Now is the time when he shall be separated from these church or temple worship practices and come voluntarily to us for further guidance and further knowledge, so he will be shown into the classrooms and be initiated into the higher orders of learning here. Thus, he will be shown, in the numerous ways which we have of doing these things here, how God can become a working part of him rather than a separate entity which must make him subservient. He thus becomes aware of his relationship, not only to this God, but to every human being who was so created by this Intelligence. Thus, he is firmly implanted upon his true pathway of evolution. So, as you saw those grey faces and forms which were coming and going through the temples on your previous visits, now you see, in this great classroom before you in this huge dimension, various buildings and centers wherein the forms which you see now do not have the grey look which they had when coming and going to the temples. They have a new luminosity. They have a spiritual viscosity which transcends and illuminates them from within because they have now discarded all their old previous thought patterns of bowing down and worshipping some strange God, or they have now ceased to be a pagan, or a pagan Christian, or a pagan Buddhist, or some other worshipful form upon the earth, for all such forms of worship are merely a higher step in the evolution of worship. Thus man comes to the place where he is not a worshipful person but now he is actually conscious that he is a part of the great Intelligent God Force, that he is moving with it toward the ultimate destination and goal which is his complete unification with this great Infinite Force.

Thus, during the remainder of this Easter service or festival upon the earth, as you know it, while it resides in the hearts and minds of hundreds of millions of earth people who have lived at one time or another upon the earth in various practices and in various cults, whether they were Druids, or whether they worshipped the great God, Amen Ra, or they worshipped Buddha, or any of the many other different personages upon the earth as intercessors to the great God, yet always this particular festival of Easter was of the same origin, of the same nature. To those who are steeped in Christian dogmas, it means the crucifixion and resurrection of the Avatar Jesus but wholly and largely, it merely means that the earth has entered into a conflux of great spiritual energies and that these are pouring into the hearts and minds of all people upon the earth. So thus it shall be with the people of the earth, as they come and go for many hundreds of years to come until the planet itself emerges into another great spiri-

1193

tual cycle which has been called the millennium when all people shall have a much larger portion of the inward working Force of God than they now possess. However, for the time being I wish for you and extend to you all of that Power and Radiance of God which I can project.

— Moses.

CHAPTER CXIV

My dear ones. It is with intense and mixed feelings and emotions that I come to you this evening and that I am able to communicate through the mind and vocal cords of two who are so dear to me. For purposes which I am considering, as these lines will be inter- jected in your book, I will omit, for the time being some of the facts which have united us together in bonds which were more than spiritual. Yes, indeed, I remember quite well when we were all together in Mecca, more than fourteen or fifteen hundred years ago. It is more than coincidence that Ruth would sell her 'iron camels', as my wife, Khadija, sold her camels that the mission of Mohammed could flourish in Islam. It is more than coincidence that you should retire to the hills, and the circle upon your forehead should arise shortly after that period. (This raised welt is called by some, the 'Eye of Mohammed'.) I will not say that Ruth is Khadija, or that Ernest is Mohammed; yet, in spirit and in being so overshadowed, who can say who is the vessel and from whence and from where does the water flow, for is it not all part of one and the same, and are we not all overshadowed with the same spirit? In the future you will be given much more of these things, but for now we must prepare for the final advent of the dedication in the closing lines of your book which will be given to you shortly by the one who, upon the earth, was called Jesus.

As this is the sabbatical or the Holy Week, at least for those who believe in Jesus, these things, too, are strongly linked, as it was explained to you, with such orders of cycles and spiritual fluxes from the Celestial Dimensions. In the Divine Mind of God all things, as they exist in law, order, and harmony, are brought into these conclusions. We, too, devote and participate in these integrated factors of relationship, so at this time we shall proceed to the Central Temple upon the planet Unarius which crowns the great Central City of Elysium, as it was called, and from this temple will be the ceremony which concerns those who are associated, either presently or in the past incarnations, with those on the planet earth; it will also concern those who have a direct and participating interest in the radiations of spiritual influx into these terrestrial domains of consciousness.

We shall take you directly to this beautiful temple. All here manifest some sort of pride or joy in believing that it is the most beautiful of all the numbers of temples in the great Centers of Unarius — and indeed it may be so. I see that you have already adjusted your vision and have your spiritual spectacles on, so we shall proceed directly up these seven great beautiful golden steps into the temple proper. As you saw when approached, it was shaped in seven semi-circular sections something like an orange which has been partially spread apart, and these various sections were hinged into a great central dome. This whole structure was of the purest sparkling translucent energy substance of a violet color and of the most intense radiance which you have yet seen. Going directly into the huge arched doorway of this first section, you become aware of some very peculiar and different things. There is a very broad aisle immediately before you which slopes down toward the great central theater-like section, and looking about you, you see that, as it was indicated from the outside, there are seven sections. Inside, however, due to the peculiar properties of the lens-like nature in the crystal substances these various seven sections have taken on an interior hue which is different from their violet appearance outside. Stemming in a clockwise fashion you can run the gamut of color, just as it was portrayed to you in the various cities which you have visited; this is also an indication that each section represents one of the Centers of Unarius and indeed this is so. Each section is filled with rows upon rows and tiers upon tiers of bench-like seats which shall be filled to capacity and overflowing on the Easter Morn.

Before each section is a huge crystal altar, also in the native color of each section. It will be from this altar that the leaders from each section shall stand and concentrate the Rays of Mind Energies with the assistance of the thousands of their fellow beings who are assisting them from the seats above. These energies shall be projected onto the great central altar which you see. Although I described it as an altar, it resembles a huge lotus of seven beautiful colored petals. Coming up into the center like the pistil of a flower is a great golden dais or a stool-like projection upon which the man Jesus will stand and deliver his dedication oration.

Now, I must pause here a moment to clear up a small point which may arouse some moral dissension in the minds of the readers of these various books. In portraying to you in the opening book of Venus, mention was made of the man Jesus and his soul mate. This quickly aroused some issue in the minds of some who read these lines, not understanding the proper balance of polarities, so that, here, in this oration, you will see both of these figures as two distinct and opposite polarities, yet, they will be contained in the same energy body. These two Individuals or these two different Polarities can function separately or together in the interchange of idea, form, structure, and energy transference into all dimensions of integration. This is a very abstract and advanced proposition and idea form, one upon which you must dwell for many years before you can hope to assimilate the extreme and advanced sacredness of its own precinct.

The idea of male or female existing in such advanced forms in these spiritual dimensions could not be tolerated or associated with the physical practices of such sexual relationships as exist in the material dimensions for purposes of procreation.

In these advanced dimensions of spiritual perception, it is the polarity concept or the function of God on two levels in two individual form structures perfectly merged in a balanced body or an energy structure — which you may call a body — which is not, of course, physical in nature but is combined of the purest and most refined essences of energy from the very Divine Mind of God Himself. I can say for every one of us here in Unarius who have not yet attained this state of relationship — and this includes myself — we are most humbly striving, if I may use that word, for this ultimate and advanced precept of consciousness. We must all attain this for some future spiritual relationship and dimension of time.

I believe at this time that we have now obtained a sufficiently enlarged view of this beautiful Temple of Elysium, and with one small exception we have not described the great vaulted dome of the ceiling which is immediately above this lotus-like altar, and, here again, there are some similarities of structures which you have previously found. Looking up through the semitranslucent material you will see that here, too, it is not quite a true dome, but which represents seven different leaves or petals, like a lotus which has been drawn together by the ends of the petals and tied with a round golden knob or a ball. These lenses of energy are likewise streaming down Radiant Energy from the Infinite Source of God around onto this great lotus-like altar. While these energies are presently neutral, yet, in some very near future, they will be catalyzed and utilized by the Mind projection into a great Radiant Flame.

From within will come the form and shape of the Leader of Unarius, the man who was also known as Jesus, who will speak to you in his own words and in the language and understanding of those who read these lines. Look forward, children, to this advent in your lives; look forward to each spiritual disclosure, to each manifestation of those who are working with you. We are most humbly subservient to the Cause and Purpose of spreading sufficient knowledge and Wisdom into the hearts and minds of the earth man, that he may, in the future millenniums to come, develop into a more spiritually minded creation and he will gradually begin to imbue within his existence the necessary spiritual factors of integration which we have found to be the true course and pattern of life.

As one who lived upon the earth and succeeded in giving some short version of spiritual integration into a book form or into such small leadership as would benefit the minds and hearts of some of my fellow men who had been misled or led astray by the false practices of altar worship and by the exploitations of the priesthoods of the different temples, so that in this service, I was able to gain some more of this Infinite Wisdom which would enable me to finally occupy such a position as it would now not be necessary to return to the earth. I realized the fallacy of changing people's minds or in attempting to do so before their time and their place, for all such spiritual revivals are usually rather short-lived; man, sooner or later, returns to the universal status quo of his present occupancy of some terrestrial dimension. As you know, the well ordered laws of rhythm in the cycles is that no man fully occupies any dimension to which he is not accustomed or that he does not 'will' himself into such a dimension of consciousness, either by lack of wisdom or a fuller understanding, so that the earth is such a point and place of this spiritual manifestation.

I have no personal message for any of those either Christian, Jew, or Moslem other than that which is contained in the books. As for personal relationships, they have all existed in their time and place but are now superseded by a much greater and more vast and Infinite Love of God, as He is manifest into a Universal Brotherhood with all mankind. Here, we do not have relatives; but all men are brothers and sisters and we are all born under one universal dominion which is the Creative Force of the Infinite Mind of the Almighty God. Until such time and place as I may return in the future, may I close by saying that you are both my personal charges; I am most happy when you are happy and I am most joyous when I am serving you both in some small way.

— Your Father Mohammed.

CHAPTER CXV

A most happy and joyous Easter infusion to you dear ones. This is the identity of a man who formerly lived on the earth and was known as St. Francis of Assisi. I have come to conduct you to the great Central Temple of Unarius and Elysium where the words or, rather, I should say, the mind radiations or inflections of the Central Mind will be directed into your channelship for interpretation into the words of the earth at your time and place. We will go there without further ado as it is almost time for Him to appear, and you must know this person who is to speak to you has been known as the Jesus who followed the Path of Light and was able to demonstrate, to some degree, the supremacy of man over his mortal self. Now, you find yourself upon the steps of the great temple which you visited with Mohammed just a short while ago, and, as a very adequate description of this place was given at that time, we shall not waste more words by adding to this description. You will also notice you are enclosed in your little bubble or the 'canopy shield of energy', and as you look about you, it is much the same as on your previous visitation except there seems to be a greater amount of pulsation or radiation. There seems to be a rather peculiar and indefinable sensation of rather a pulsating nature within you and even though the shield is strongly constructed, were you outside of the shield at this time, you might suffer severe psychic shock because your present psychic body is not sufficiently constituted with these higher forms of radiant energy infusions which would enable you to pass through these dimensions without this repercussion in your psychic centers.

Now, we will step within the temple and you will see the cause for all of this tremendous radiant agita-

1201

tion which you feel about you. As it was formerly empty, now it is filled to its utmost capacity with the radiant and beautiful forms of my fellow Unariuns. This temple seems to be even larger than it was on your previous visitation, which is somewhat of the peculiarities of these structures; they seem to expand or contract according to the needs of the time and the place. I might also mention that most of the people who are thus assembled here were, at one time, upon the dimension or planet of earth, and they are largely concerned with this period of the Easter Festival which is being portrayed in hundreds of millions of earth minds at this time. It is their purpose in the understanding of the earth man and his life at this most propitious and opportune time to add to and project the Radiant Energy into the minds of these millions of upturned hearts and faces.

Now, as you see that the ceremony is about to begin, I will pause temporarily after the description of the building up of the great flame upon the central golden platform in the middle of the lotus-like altar which was previously described.

As before, there starts the tremendous upsurging sing-song chanting energies, something like a most sacred and holy mantrum which begins; and now, you are seeing great waves of beautiful Radiant Energy which seem to roll down over the heads of the assembled multitudes. They are cascading into this great central altar of the lotus-like flower and are being absorbed into what now appears to be a huge radiant ball of energy with an inward flame of the Radiant Energies which are being absorbed into it. Soon there will appear within this, the personage whom we call the Central Mind or the Moderator of Unarius. He is the Spiritual Person of the man who was formerly known as Jesus upon the earth. Now, as you see, and as you have been told, He is actually not just a single person, but a perfectly blended and merged combination of two polarities — his soul mate and himself who have joined in this spiritual union at this time so they may be of greater and more unified purpose in the projection and in the assistance of these things.

I would add here, too, a note that during this month and particularly this week, we have been most busy in various initiation services and ceremonies. Many have come into our dimensions of consciousness from the lower spiritual or astral worlds to be initiated into our way of life. We have held such services or ceremonies which were most suitable and conducive to added sources of such Radiant Energies as they may be suitably impounded into the minds of the earth people at this time. Now, it is almost to the point of projection where this Central Mind will enter into the conflux. As you have been watching, those who were in the leadership of the various sections of the other Centers of Unarius are now standing in their proper positions, each before His altar which is in front of the great Lotus Altar. Now, within the center of the great flame you see the form and shape of something which is very radiant and very beautiful. It does assume some proportions or form of a human being, yet this must be so in your own mind for better purposes of conceiving such things. This form will appear quite differently in some respects to those who are assembled in this great congregation. But for your purposes or the purposes of better assimilation to the minds of those who read these lines, we can project to you this form which is somewhat like that of yourself; rather, that it is larger or taller and that it is more sublimely proportioned. It is indeed a great mass of pulsating Radiant Energy of the most intense and beautiful nature.

The intensity of the energies has now reached almost climactic proportions; the flame has begun to subside and leave there this very beautiful and magnificent form or proportion of the Central Mind, the personality of this Leader of Unarius. You will pardon my difficulty somewhat with the earth words which lead directly to the unproportions of personal identity, as we associate such things much differently than they are done upon the earth. Now, I must be quiet and hushed for a moment for soon He will radiate through the channel of your mind the words, or the thoughts, rather, which He has brought with Him for the purpose and the time. Do not expect Him to talk in the language of Biblical times or that He shall impose parabolical forms or interpretations. His purpose today is to give a rather brief form and message of dedication for your services in writing the books and into the book itself that it may further the progress and betterment of mankind.

For myself, I am most humbly observant of my capacity in helping you fulfill such works and to the furtherance and betterment of mankind — and so until the time when we shall be in contact with each other, other than in the spiritual way, I will stand by ever ready to assist you.

— Francis.

CHAPTER CXVI

My love to you dear ones; this is a most joyous
and happy occasion that once again into the hearts
and minds of my fellow man I can come to you in something other than a symbol or a semblance of some spiritual power, and that I can reside again in your hearts
and minds as a person who is, in his own way, serving
the Most High God Forces, and into the channels
which are most beneficient to my fellow man. As these
things are brought about into the consciousness and
into the minds and hearts of those who are in the lower
terrestrial orders of existence, it was so, that two
thousand years ago an individual proved to his fellow
man that he need not fear the most commonly accepted
forms of such things as were called death, or material
orders of existence, that he was indeed a creation of
the most Infinite Nature which was always ready to
ascend into the spiritual dimensions, and that the
will and prerogative of this most Infinite Mind of God
was always in contact with him in direct proportion
to all that he was to be.

It has been with great pleasure that I have watched
you come and go into these Centers and that you and
sister were able to add from time to time many things
of great value, many facets of interpretation which
would be of great service to your fellow man. It has
also been that these things were, as you told, ordered
within the dimension of time and place of so many numerous cycles of interpretation, and that coming and
going into these great Spiritual Dimensions, not only in
the time and place of your present life, but into such
times and places of the past, that these things became
a great plan with you, a complete realization for a
setting aside of the 'self' so that these things could
bring great blessings into the hearts and minds of those

who would be patient enough to read of these things, to study them, and to observe their immediate effects within their own personalities. We can say to these sundry and numerous and diverse personalities that we have added much in the way of spiritual energies to the furtherance and the purpose of these works. And there resides within the concept of our minds something which can be termed a great universe of spiritual energy which shall flow outwardly into the minds and hearts of all those who pursue these lines and to pursue the lines and channels of thinking which will be set up within them upon reading these lines, as you must know of all these things and many more before you can truly rise to the consciousness of the Higher Self. To those who are steeped in the fundamentalism of the earth and that you have been told that I shall come upon a shining cloud with thunder and lightning and with a Host of Angels, do not be disappointed that I shall not appear to you thusly. Rather, it should be that I shall come in the quietness of your inner moments with the communion of self and that I do not come as a person, but rather with an influx of the most Divine Essences of the Inward God Self. This is of yourself, like that of your fellow man, your own inward consciousness, your own realization of what is called the Christ, or the Divine Self and purposes of man. Thus, it shall be that you shall come in contact with the Creative Force which was so most divinely inspired and motivated in the highest and completeness of all things. I am One who has come to learn something of a more expanded nature of the time and purpose, and place of, not only my own capacities and realizations, but of those with whom I am presently working and so occupied with their well-being and their furtherance into spiritual dimensions. Surely, of all these things then, there must constantly arise within us, from time to time, all of the inspiration and creative measures of God's most Infinite Mind, to supersede the needs of the self or the selfish being to thus be integrated into a common union, the bonds of a Universal Brotherhood which is, not only terrestrial in nature, but comes and goes as do the tides into the numerous terrestrial and spiritual dimensions of man's consciousness; into the farthest corners of the remotest universes, do these great waves and influxes of this spiritual Brotherhood ascend and descend from the most Divine Mind of God, so that we all come into our own proper time in our own proper place; and thus, you see about you upon the earth the swarms of humanity who are struggling for something of that inward sight, that inward selflessness, and that realization which will place them in a unified position with the inward workings of the most high Consciousness.

We have all assembled here today, as we have done so many times in the past, for some particular observance or ceremony which was most directive to the inflow of these Divine High Essences; and we shall never cease to do so upon any particular occasion when such need has arisen or the time is most advantageous for such dispensations. Thus, it is today, so it will be in the future, that we shall never cease to do these things, not only with yourself but with any of or the numerous channels which may arise within the terrestrial dimensions of mankind.

To the future, may I say that many of these radiant Personages that you see about you will descend into these terrestrial dimensions in their proper time and place and add to the universal store of Infinite Wisdom in their proper relationships; and these things shall all bring man into a closer harmony and realization with the most high self, with the most divine purposes of God's Infinite Mind and his relationship to the great Brotherhoods in the Spiritual Dimensions.

In conclusion, may I say to you, one and all: Become completely dedicated to the purpose of realization; that in this realization you become selfless, that you become integrated, that you are also in such relationships with your fellow man which will bring you into such unified harmonious conclusions with all things which God has bestowed within you. These things are not born of selfish desires nor of things which must be set about you for your own use, such purposes as concern the self; but only through this self can you express outwardly that which is within you and that all things of the outward nature must be so related with the inward nature that they, too, serve the purpose of the outwardness into the furtherance of all things in great and universal concepts of the Infinite Brotherhood of man. So thus it shall be.

May I also add to this my own personal Blessings of Love, of fulfillment, of all of the things of self-realization which will bring to you the bounty of this Infinite God Self. I shall always remain with you, and as it was so promised, so it shall be fulfilled that the Comforter, as it has sometimes been called, shall be there to fulfill the need and the time of the hour, and that this Comforter is the Highest of the High Self Within; and you should seek out this Comforter to attain a higher realization with this Inward Higher Self. for this is indeed the doorway into Infinite Concept of the Most High and Infinite God. Until such further time, be happy and joyous in the conclusion of all things about you; that these are all proper in their time and in their place, and fulfill their own particular destiny; that these things are all of the Infinite nature and that they are of an Infinite purpose. They have an Infinite evolution and so they shall serve mankind wherever he does come into whatever evolution of consciousness he so ascends or descends. He shall add to all of these things of his most High Self and thus come into the true Spiritual Kingdom of his own dimension. May this most God-like nature be always with you, within you, and upon you.

— Amen.

note –

These transmissions were received and recorded during 1957 – '58 but were not printed or published until 1964, thus some mentions made regarding earths activities were in reference to that period of time; also many prophecies given then, have since come to pass.

———

For complete list of other books by same author:

Write to

Unarius Science of Life

P. O. Box 157,

Montrose, Calif.